THE ROUGH-SHOOTER'S HANDBOOK

THE ROUGH-SHOOTER'S HANDBOOK

Guy N. Smith

THE BOYDELL PRESS

First published 1986 by The Boydell Press
an imprint of Boydell & Brewer Ltd
PO Box 9, Woodbridge, Suffolk IP12 3DF

British Library Cataloguing in Publication Data

Smith, Guy N.
    The rough-shooter's handbook.
    1. Hunting—Great Britain
    I. Title
    799.2'13   SK185
ISBN 0-85115-449-2

Printed and bound in Great Britain at
The Camelot Press Ltd, Southampton

Contents

Acknowledgements

The British Association for Shooting and Conservation for allowing me to reproduce from their brochure and for helping me with numerous queries.

M. G. Walker & Son, Game Farmers, The Lodge, Four Ashes, Enville, Stourbridge, Worcs., for their advice on large scale pheasant rearing.

David Cluett, for supplying me with photographs relating to gamekeeping.

Lance Smith, for the majority of illustrations.

Calvin Williams, for providing illustrations relating to wildfowling.

*This book is dedicated to
my shooting companions over the last thirty years*

Introduction

The purpose of this book is to help the enthusiastic sportsman to find somewhere to shoot. The problems are widespread and complex, the solution is not easy. We live in the age of cheque-book shooting; if one's bank balance is considerable then one only has to consult the classified columns of the sporting press to locate a day's first class driven pheasants at around £250 or perhaps £12 per bird. Package deals include duck-flighting, inland goose-shooting, even an afternoon on the moors after grouse. If your bank account can stand it, the possibilities are endless. You may even decide to go to Spain after partridge, or to Hungary and shoot 300 pheasants in a day, with perhaps the odd wild boar thrown in.

Unfortunately those options are for the minority and the average shooting man must seek and find his sport at home. That sport need not be inferior, it is the quality of the shooting that counts; a wily cock pheasant, worked up with a dog in rough terrain, can provide a testing shot equal to your £12 bird on a driven shoot. The satisfaction will be that much greater on a d.i.y. shoot because whatever you achieve will have been entirely due to your own efforts.

The first step is to weigh up the possibilities and decide exactly what kind of shooting you require. The choice is a relatively wide one and basically those open to you are:

1. renting a small shoot of your own
2. renting a larger acreage and forming a syndicate to meet the costs
3. relying on invitations from friends
4. obtaining permission to shoot rabbits, pigeons and vermin
5. coastal wildfowling

We shall look at each of these in turn throughout this book, but first the beginner must be made aware how much and why the shooting spectrum has changed over the past two decades and how all this has affected the focal point of all field sports – the habitat of the quarry.

The sporting scene began to undergo a drastic change as far back as the end of the First World War. Until then, the coastal haunts of the vast flocks of wildfowl which wintered on our shores were the domain of the professional wildfowler. He relied upon large bags for his livelihood, whether shot in a sporting fashion with shoulder gun or punt gun, or caught in the decoys which were fashionable in those days. He would market his duck, geese and wading birds and perhaps cut reeds or catch shellfish during the summer season. But the advent of the motor car was destined to change all this. Soon the visiting gentlemen fowlers were to appear on the scene, converging on that Mecca for wildfowlers, Wells-next-the-Sea in Norfolk. The flighting geese, which hitherto had come to accept the scattered band of local gunners, were now faced with a barrage of fire, morning and night. They learned to fly higher, out of gunshot, but even this did not deter the optimistic shooters. Larger bores, heavier shot – it was a tradition at Wells that you 'had a go'.

The ultimate result was that before hostilities resumed in 1939 the geese at Wells and Holkham had had enough. They moved on, found quieter places further north on the vast marshes of the Wash and Skegness. The fowlers followed them. Not content with lying in ambush along the sea wall, greedy shooters began digging-in out on the mudflats where the geese roosted and blasting them as they returned at deep dusk, even harassing them on moonlight nights. Over-shooting and out-of-range shooting was to sound the death knell of wildfowling. Conducted in a sportsmanlike manner there would have been, and still would be, wildfowling on all of our coastal marshes.

But there are other factors which have combined to reduce our quarry species and diminish their habitat and it is well worth looking at some of these in an attempt to understand why wild game is not nearly so prolific as it once was, and why land which we once might have shot over is no longer available to us.

1. Chemical sprays

Without any doubt herbicides and pesticides have contributed to the decline of our wild life. The partridges were the first to suffer, along with our birds of prey. Insects comprise the most important part of a gamebird's diet and chemical sprays have wiped it out indiscriminately. Only a year or two ago 150 dead hares were picked up within a radius of one and a half miles in Oxfordshire, the victims of paraquat spraying. I also read a very frightening report of a Springer spaniel which had been retrieving pigeons from a field of laid barley. On returning home its owner discovered ears of corn embedded in its flesh like darts. He removed them, but within a few weeks cancerous sores developed and in due course the animal had to be destroyed. These are just two examples of what chemicals are doing to the environment.

Why are there chemicals on the land? Farmers have been indoctrinated into their use over the years and the discovery that they could cultivate weedless acres encouraged them to use these sprays even more extensively. Gradually, the evil built up until realisation came too late. Now, thanks to such excellent dedicated organisations as the Friends of the Earth, the public have been made aware of what is happening. Some farmers have realised their mistake and have reverted to organic farming. Hopefully HRH the Prince of Wales has set the trend by a return to former farming methods on part of his own estates. It is estimated that by 1990 20 per cent of our farmland will be farmed organically. We can only hope that it is not too late and that our wildlife may yet be saved.

2. Strawburning

Little more than a decade ago pyromania swept our countryside in the form of stubble burning. In those parts of the country where livestock was not farmed extensively, and hence straw was not needed for bedding, it was decided to burn the straw on the fields rather than bale it. The excuse was put forward that straw bales were not worth the string used to tie them. In effect it was the easy way out for large farmers who were making fortunes out of subsidies anyway and did not need the small remuneration to be derived from baling, transporting and selling their straw.

This resulted in hedgerows being burned, the atmosphere being polluted, and at least one horrific road crash caused by thick smoke akin to a pea-souper fog. Yet this lunacy continued in spite of the fact that in certain parts of the country stockmen were crying out for straw. In addition to its conventional use for bedding for animals, straw can be used for insulation for houses, and cheap fuel if compressed into bricks. But this was ignored and those few remaining patches of habitat were either burned or the occupants driven away by the smoke. Young gamebirds were incinerated and even those who escaped were unlikely to return to a charred countryside.

A public outcry resulted in legislation, but instead of banning this indiscriminate burning all that resulted were restrictions. So the blaze continues during the late summer months; sporting potential has been destroyed for the sake of a few rolls of baler twine.

3. Increased grassland and grain 'plains'

'Mountains' of grain, meat, butter, milk etc., have accumulated over the years and nobody really knows what is the purpose of this surplus. Whatever reasons are given, there is no doubt that the environment has suffered as a result. Once our agricultural scene was made up of small fields, thick hedgerows which offered cover and food for wildlife. Now the majority of these are gone, traditional hedges uprooted to make larger fields so that excess grain and meat can be reared which nobody apparently wants. Without the huge subsidies paid to these farmers they would almost certainly be the paupers of the land; no other business could flourish whilst producing surplus goods.

Thus we have undergone a desecration of our natural cover. In fairness, there is a scheme in its infancy whereby farmers are receiving grants to *plant* hedges, but once again has realisation come too late? Acres of grassland are of little benefit to game, grazed too short to provide natural cover and offering little in the way of food. Certainly such barren areas are no good to the shooting man and if the stubble is being burned immediately after harvest then those fields will be devoid of game.

Gone is the old-fashioned method of pleaching hedges, to be replaced by a ravenous mechanical monster that gobbles up the excess growth and leaves us with mile after mile of unsightly hedgerows. The hedges are low and sparse, the chewed-up cuttings deposited in the stools which should, in theory, rot down. What actually happens is that this waste stifles the growth and over a long period the foliage will suffer. So we have the worst of two evils; either the hedges are bulldozed out and removed forever or else they are machine-cut in such a way that they offer neither cover nor food for wildlife. We can only hope that the new hedge-planting programme proves to be a long term salvation and that once again our wildlife will have some kind of habitat in these barren parts of the country.

The hedges today are low and sparse. (Photo: Lance Smith)

4. The march of civilisation

All of us are only too well aware how conurbations have swallowed up the countryside which we knew in our childhood. Where we once roamed over fields there are now housing estates, industrial estates and major roads. The once familiar scene is often totally unrecognisable.

Unfortunately there is very little we can do about this, except to lobby local councillors when there is the remotest hint of building being allowed in Green Belt areas.

5. Quarrying

Quarrying is like the bubonic plague. It spreads and kills all before it. It is often a devious process that begins with a small quarry and expands slowly and relentlessly. Beware when local woodlands are felled. If re-planting is delayed it could be that the owners have quarrying in mind. They need planning permission but this can slip through virtually unnoticed, perhaps only a small notice in the local paper. The countryside will be scarred for years to come, another habitat gone forever. The added threat is that building permission might be given to the land after it has remained an unsightly

Quarrying is like the bubonic plague, it spreads and kills all before it.
(Photo: Lance Smith)

cancer on the landscape for so many years. We must do everything possible to prevent unnecessary building in our countryside; it is not a question of shortage of homes for there are thousands of acres of derelict ground in Britain, around the towns and cities, where a modern housing estate would enhance the locality. It is sheer greed on behalf of some unscrupulous landowner. Be on your guard where permission is applied for to build two or three 'executive-style houses'. Be sure that others will follow in due course.

6. Afforestation

Trees are better than bricks and mortar but nevertheless large tracts of commercial afforestation are detrimental to wildlife in any area. Following the Second World War a massive forestry programme was embarked upon in Britain. Vast areas of upland terrain and moorland were planted with symmetrical rows of coniferous trees. The heather which had once been the territory of blackgame and grouse was gone and the birds sought another habitat elsewhere. Overcrowding led to disease, numbers dwindled and the grouse population declined. The birds were deprived of their staple diet, new shoots of heather.

In fairness to the Forestry Commission, however, they are true conservationists and endeavour to protect wildlife wherever possible, and their contribution to the environment is invaluable. The shooting man has gained because the Commission lease many hectares of sporting rights which otherwise would not be available to the sportsman of modest means. We shall deal with this in detail in a later chapter.

7. The Wildlife and Countryside Act 1981

In effect this is a hotch-potch of well-meaning but misguided legislation. The sportsman has suffered in that all wading birds, with the exception of snipe and golden plover, have been given protection. The wildfowler's main loss has been the redshank and the curlew, both excellent sporting and eating birds whose numbers are *increasing*. Their removal from the quarry list can in no way be justified.

8. Purchase of land by conservation societies

Another erosion of good shooting land has been brought about by the purchase of land, mostly marshland, by conservation bodies whose main aim is the cessation of shooting on those acreages. Traditional wildfowling has come to a halt but ultimately the wildlife itself will suffer. Corvines will breed and multiply without culling, and in the end this attempt to conserve will have been defeated. Every species must have a predator if it is to maintain a healthy stock and man plays a vital role in keeping the balance of nature. A no-killing programme is false conservation.

9. The 'anti's'

Whatever you enjoy doing there is always somebody who wants to put a stop to it. That is a fact of life in this modern day and age and fieldsports have not escaped this silly disease. However, the latest moves are decidedly sinister, involving damage to property, violence, and now death-threats. A minority have become criminals, involving themselves in issues which they do not understand and apparently have no wish to. They are the ones who inflict the most cruelty on animals, releasing species into the wild where they cannot adjust, condemning them to starvation and death. These fringe groups have a touch of the Ku-Klux-Klan about them except that they don't wear a sheet and a silly hat. Not yet, anyway.

Perhaps I have portrayed a picture of deepening gloom but I feel that it is best that the sportsman or prospective sportsman realises fully what he is up against. Things definitely aren't what they used to be but that does not mean that everything is going to come to a stop. It merely means that the challenge is that much greater. The search for shooting by the novice is a daunting prospect but it can be overcome. If you have the will then there is surely a way.

Finally, before you embark upon the search to find somewhere to shoot, you must ask yourself honestly why you want to shoot. Simply to go out and kill for the sake of killing, albeit a legitimate quarry species, is immoral and inexcusable. You shoot for two reasons; either to kill something to eat (or to pass it on to someone who will enjoy eating it), or because the quarry is a predatory species detrimental to gamebirds, wildlife in general, or farm stock. If you just fancy firing a gun then you should contact your local clay pigeon club and go and bust a few clays. Clays have no part in this book, for it is a book for the hunter.

I admit to being a 'pot-hunter'. My foremost reason for taking a gun out, either on my own smallholding or the adjoining land which I lease, is to bring home food for my family. No other reason, only that I like to kill as humanely and in as sportsmanlike a way as possible.

Game is the only meat we eat. We do not eat red meat or any domestically-reared animal with the exception of the occasional free-range cockerel or turkey simply because wild meat is low in cholesterol. Likewise we avoid any foodstuffs containing additives and all the produce we grow is organic; we do not even use chemical weedkiller on the drive. So game is important to us; if we could not obtain it then we should eat all vegetarian foods.

My wife and children often accompany me shooting. They are all keen that the sport should flourish. Killing a pheasant or guineafowl in full flight is far kinder than grabbing a chicken in the henhouse and pulling its neck. The former has a sporting chance; the latter experiences terror and smells death. That is what it is all about, killing for food as our ancestors did thousands of years ago. Evolution has not changed one's natural instinct to hunt.

That is why we must persevere in our attempts to find somewhere to shoot. The right to carry a gun and to kill for food must not be denied us. And if I am successful in helping just one or two readers in their quest for shooting then the writing of this book will have been worthwhile.

I feel that there is still a great future for our sport.

Guy N. Smith,
Black Hill,
Clun.

CHAPTER ONE

Necessary Preparations

Shotgun certificates

Before you can purchase, borrow, take a gun out shooting, you must have a shotgun certificate. This replaced the old 10/- gun licence which anyone could buy over the counter in a post office.

There should be no problem in obtaining a shotgun certificate. Your local police station will supply you with an application form which you must fill in. If you have had any court convictions then you must state them, with the exception of minor motoring offences. These will be taken into consideration by the police when granting certificates; obviously the aim is to keep guns out of the hands of criminals. Unfortunately the policy seems to be to impose restrictions upon the legitimate gun owner. Criminals will always obtain firearms, licensing will not affect them.

However, if you have a clean record you should not encounter any problems. I have read of cases where it seems that the police are deliberately looking for a reason not to grant a certificate but these are the exception rather than the rule. It is your right to own a shotgun if you so wish.

Personally I have received only co-operation from the law and my renewals have always gone through automatically by post without an officer calling to see me.

Fill your application form in carefully, read the questions and answer them truthfully. An inadvertent mistake can cause confusion and delay. Then either take the form, together with the appropriate fee, to your local police station or post it to the firearms department at county police headquarters. Until you receive your certificate you cannot buy or use a gun.

Buying a gun

There are many detailed books on the subject of which gun and cartridges to use, and as this book is designed primarily to help the reader find somewhere to shoot, this is merely a brief mention of ballistics. At this stage the beginner is concerned with choosing a gun to use in the early stages and will, in all probability, change it for something to suit his personal requirements when he becomes more proficient.

Most important of all the gun must *fit* you. Like a suit of clothes you must feel comfortable, be able to mount it easily and swing with it. In no way must it feel cumbersome; it must be an extension of your own body.

I started my own shooting career with a .410, as have my own children, but I feel that this weapon has its limitations. The pattern is small, the effective killing range is only 20/25 yards and, to be honest, you need to be an accomplished shot to kill consistently with it. There is nothing more discouraging for a youngster than to find he can't hit anything. Far better to start with a lightweight 28-bore, progressing to a 20-bore after a couple of years or so.

I checked with my local firearms department on the question of my eight-year-old son carrying a .410. He was too young to apply for a certificate and, anyway, my policy is that children should learn to carry an *empty* gun in a safe manner for the first few years whilst they find out what the sport is all about. No way would I tolerate young boys accompanying me shooting with a loaded gun; they must learn the basics of the sport first, appreciate that there is a lot more to it than simply firing a gun. The police informed me that this was quite in order and my son was entitled to carry a loaded gun under *adult supervision*, and on land owned by myself or where I had the shooting rights.

The idea worked well and as a special 'treat' I carry a .410 cartridge in my pocket and at some time during the proceedings I allow my son to fire his gun, usually at some inanimate object such as a sheet of plastic. The process of learning must be gradual, along with quarry identification and the ways of the countryside.

Anyone over the age of fifteen is advised to start with a lightweight 12-bore, preferably with improved cylinder and half-choke barrels. Judging range is a vital starting point and the temptation to take long shots must be resisted. I rarely shoot at anything over 40 yards even with a full-choke barrel. Apart from the fact that I abhor wounding, valuable time can be wasted hunting for 'runners', and also I hate wasting cartridges. To me a box of cartridges is the equivalent of a packet of seeds on the smallholding; I expect a fair return for my outlay.

I have always favoured a good sound English gun. A personal choice and I am sure that many of the imported guns that we see advertised today are equal to the home-made product, but to me a gun is a very personal possession and there is nobody to beat the British craftsman. You don't have to pay an extortionate price for your gun. Study the classified columns of the sporting press carefully and go for a good sound second-hand hammerless non-ejector, nothing fancy. Before you buy it, get it checked over by a gunmaker or somebody who really knows something about guns. Look after it, clean it after each outing and it will serve you for many years to come.

The complete novice would do well to try his hand at a few clays first, not that I am an advocate of clay-shooting, but they are handy for getting used to shooting at a moving target. A shooting school is best because you will have the added benefit of an instructor coaching you. It will take you some time to break your first clay, even longer to smash them consistently, but you need to know at the very outset where you are going wrong. Otherwise you will continue to make the same mistake and will not hit anything. The most important fact of all is to learn to swing with your target and to keep on swinging after you have fired, otherwise every shot will be behind.

Once you have mastered this it will become a habit; a bird will rise, you will keep both eyes firmly fixed on it, swing and pull. It is all a matter of practice.

Hammer or hammerless gun?

This is an argument that has raged since the introduction of the hammerless shotgun. If you are concerned with the safety factor then it is best to understand how a hammerless gun is made 'safe'. The safety-catch merely locks the triggers, otherwise the weapon is on full cock once the breech is closed. You are relying on a mechanical device; a severe blow to the weapon, dropping it or knocking it over, *could* discharge it.

On the other hand we have a positive and negative situation with the hammer gun. If the hammers are pulled back it will fire; if they are lowered there is no way it can go off.

The argument often presented in respect of the hammer gun's safety angle is that of lowering the hammers on a loaded gun. Cold or inexperienced fingers could slip and the gun go off. However, it all depends upon the gun itself. Many weapons are so made that one can open the breech first and then lower the hammers, in which case there is no danger whatsoever. My first hammer gun did not operate like that; there was no room for the breech-lever to open the gun whilst it was at full cock.

I merely make observations and am totally unbiased. It certainly takes a second or so longer to cock your gun when a bird flushes than to push a safety-catch forward, and it would be unwise to walk with the weapon fully cocked.

It is a matter of personal choice. Many of the great shots of Victorian and Edwardian days used hammer guns.

Cartridges

Whatever cartridge you use, it must suit the gun in which it is fired. I remember many years ago purchasing a box of top quality 2½-inch cartridges and using them one afternoon in my 3-inch magnum. The misses were

11

unbelievable; a cock pheasant clattered up beneath my feet and survived both barrels. Three mallard coming in to land with their paddles down escaped unscathed. Then, a few days later, I went out with my lightweight game gun and using those same cartridges killed everything I shot at!

My advice to the beginner is not to become involved in ballistics. One reads that a certain cartridge will kill cleanly at 40 yards and is suitable for duck or hares, another is ideal for driven game, etc. In effect, if your gun suits you and the cartridge patterns well in your gun then it doesn't matter what the quarry is provided it is within range.

For preference I use a 1¹/₈ oz game load, size 7 in the right barrel, 5 in the left. Later in the season when the birds are wilder I use 5s in both. My cartridges are paper-cased and I have seldom had any trouble with swollen cases. I find that plastic cases are inclined to slip out of my cartridge belt when I put it on or take it off, and either roll all over the floor or, worse, drop in the mud. Also the printing rubs off and I find that I have half a belt of anonymous cartridges of which I am uncertain of the shot sizes. The purist will swear by crimped cases but I don't think it makes that much difference if you are a reasonable shot. Too many misses are blamed on either gun or cartridges whereas in the majority of cases the fault lies with the shooter. .

The beginner should test a few cartridges in his new gun by firing at a sheet of newspaper pinned up on a board and get an idea which brands and shot sizes suit the gun best. Don't be led astray by the myth that the heavier the load and the larger the shot size the more you will kill. Certainly a magnum load will kill further than a game load but it is not a licence to take long shots. Aim at killing cleanly at 35 to 40 yards, which a good game load is perfectly capable of doing. A heavier load will mash your birds up and render them inedible.

A few years ago I purchased some clay cartridges, 1¹/₈ oz load of 7¹/₂ shot. They killed pigeon superbly but I found that there were an awful lot of pellets in the bodies even with head shots. The pattern was just too good!

Clothing

I maintain that the three basic requirements for shooting are a good gun, reliable cartridges and suitable clothing. Anything other than a game bag and cartridge belt becomes an unnecessary encumbrance. One can be tempted by adverts for various accessories but the majority of them are superfluous. It is the beginner struggling to find form in the field who purchases these 'extras'.

The right clothing is important, though. I regard a hat as imperative. Not only does it protect the head from extremes of climate but it serves as camouflage, particularly where pigeon and duck are concerned. Probably the best headgear of all is the soft deerstalker with flaps. The flaps can be handy to protect your ears on bitterly cold days and the peak at either end shelters both your face and your neck. It is fashionable in the shooting field without being ostentatious.

A jacket needs to be comfortable so that your shooting is in no way impeded. Perhaps a light showerproof one for early in the season when the weather is inclined to be warm, and a slightly heavier waterproof and thornproof one for the winter months when you are likely to encounter heavy storms. If you are wet and cold you will not shoot well.

When buying a waterproof jacket check that it is ventilated. I once had one that had no ventilation whatsoever and I got wetter on the inside than the heaviest storm could have soaked me without a jacket!

Large pockets are handy but check that you do not inadvertently tuck the flaps in. The waterproof material will hold water inside those pockets and this can be most unpleasant.

Trousers should be light, durable and fairly weatherproof. For wet days you can always take along a pair of slip-on waterproofs but these can be uncomfortable if worn all day. Moleskins are about the best; they are thick enough to keep the cold out, are fairly showerproof and are a comfortable soft material. Failing that, I would go for cords. But *not* jeans. Jeans will soak through at the first shower and cling wetly to your legs.

Good footwork is essential to good marksmanship, so footwear is an important item. There are innumerable varieties on the market, it depends which kind you are most comfortable in. I have always been used to wearing good old-fashioned wellington boots and nowadays they make them in nice sporty green colours. My local ironmonger sells synthetic wellies at £5 a pair and one pair, barring barbed-wire accidents, usually lasts me twelve months and that includes wearing them for farmwork!

Some may prefer a shorter, lighter boot. Of course, leather is the best material but it entails a lot of work. One cannot throw them into the cupboard at the end of a day's shooting and leave them there until next time. They require applications of dubbin, no small amount of elbow grease, and are at their best when well-worn.

It is what you are comfortable in that counts most.

Dogs

Nobody should shoot without a dog that is capable of finding a wounded bird and retrieving it. On the other hand, you are worse off with an unruly dog that does not know its job.

The choice of dog is a wide one and much thought must be given to it. There are different dogs for different types of shooting. For instance, pointers are ideal for walking up grouse on the moors, the trained dog standing like a statue and pointing when it scents a covey rather than rushing forward and flushing the birds before you are within shot. Perhaps the best all-round shooting dog is the labrador. I had two; Remus, my first one, lived to nearly sixteen and was still working right up to the end, and Simon made it to seventeen. They are good workers, strong, and will suit either the rough-shooter or the wildfowler.

Four years ago I changed to a Springer spaniel. The reason for this was largely due to the terrain over which I shoot; steep hillsides covered in gorse and bracken, thick woodlands with impenetrable barriers of brambles. There is virtually nothing which a spaniel will not face and they are excellent in water also.

However, a spaniel is like no other gundog. From the moment it is taken out of the kennel its instinct is to hunt. It will investigate every blade of grass, every frond of bracken, and it will not rest until the end of the day. Just watching Muffin work makes me feel exhausted! I had her as a pup and only gave her the basic training on purpose. My requirements of her are to hunt thick cover and flush birds, to retrieve and to return to me when I whistle. Apart from that she is a free agent and I have certainly shot more over her than I did over the labradors.

I would not dream of taking her to an organised shoot. Indeed, I never intended her to sit during drives. On those occasions when I do not want her ranging freely I have a long lead and chain attached to a loop around my

The spaniel's instinct is to hunt. (Photo: Lance Smith)

cartridge belt. Now, the first piece of advice I would give any novice is not to attach a dog to your person. Many years ago I learned the hard way when Remus pulled me into a deep ditch during a hare drive! However, the lead was part of Muffin's training and she makes no attempt either to work or run-in once tethered. It is a very convenient arrangement.

I have no objection to a dog that runs-in to shot provided they do not go wild. Indeed, on more than one occasion Muffin has virtually arrived on the scene with a bird thudding down in front of her nose. If it is a runner it stands less chance of eluding her and unnecessary suffering may be saved. The sooner a dog is on the scent, the better. Picking-up at the end of a drive usually means that the runners have got a good start.

The beginner is advised to start with a pup from a good working pedigree. One trained by oneself is always preferable to the dog trained by somebody

Extended lead attached to cartridge belt. (Photo: Lance Smith)

15

else but it is best to seek advice beforehand. The foundation for the whole of the dog's working life will be laid in its first year.

Most important of all, your dog is your companion, one who will share your successes and failures, and therefore deserves the best treatment you can give it. After a cold wet day it should be dried off immediately on your return home, fed and cared for before you turn your attention to your next task, the cleaning of your gun. That hot bath and waiting meal must come third in your list of priorities.

Shooting seasons and quarry identification

It is the duty of every sportsman to determine just what species are legal quarry and when he can shoot them.

Listed below are the shooting seasons of various game:

Pheasant	1 October–1 February
Partridge	1 September–1 February
Grouse	12 August–10 December
Blackgame	20 August–10 December
Ptarmigan	12 August–10 December (Scotland only)
Capercaillie	1 October–31 January
Hare	There is no close season but hares may only be shot by the occupier of land or those authorised by him and may not be offered for sale from 1 March to 31 July. *Hares may only be shot by those holding a game licence.*
Geese and Duck	1 September–31 January, but on coastal areas below the high water mark of ordinary spring tides they may be shot up to 20 February.
Snipe	12 August–31 January
Woodcock	1 October–31 January in England and Wales 1 September–31 January in Scotland
Moorhen, Coot and Golden Plover	1 September–31 January

Rabbit, pigeon and vermin species may be shot at any time. It should be noted that whilst corvines can be killed at any time, ravens are protected by law and it is the duty of the sportsman to learn to identify this bird by its larger size and deep-throated 'cronk'.

All birds of prey are protected.

It is the duty of the shooting man to be able to identify all legitimate species which may be shot. If in doubt, do not shoot and take steps to find out what bird you saw. You must incorporate ornithology with shooting and learn the habits of birds and animals other than those which you shoot. Conservation and shooting go hand in hand.

Game licences

You need a game licence, obtainable from most post offices in the United Kingdom at a cost of £6.00, in order to shoot game. Failure to comply with this may result in prosecution and you could, as a result, lose your shotgun certificate. Game licences run from 1 August to 31 July and it is advisable to buy one before the commencement of the shooting season. As already stated, you need a licence to shoot hares but not rabbits.

The BASC (The British Association for Shooting and Conservation)

The novice has obtained his shotgun certificate and game licence, chosen a gun and cartridges which suit him, purchased some adequate clothing and trained his dog. But there is still one important step to take before he sets out on the search for some shooting. It is the duty of every shooting man, novice or experienced shot, to belong to the BASC in this day and age when his sport is under attack from many quarters.

In 1908 Stanley Duncan, a far-sighted wildfowler, recognised the increasing threat to the sport and formed WAGBI (the Wildfowlers' Association of Great Britain and Ireland). The Association grew, became actively involved in conservation as well as taking an interest in all shooting sports and developing services to cater for the needs of its increasing membership. In June 1981, the name was changed to the British Association for Shooting and Conservation and now has a membership of more than 60,000. The headquarters remained at Marford Mill, Rossett, near Wrexham in Clwyd.

For seven successive years now there has been a substantial increase in membership yet out of some 700,000 shotgun certificate holders this only represents a mere 12 per cent. In other words, non-members are riding on the backs of the faithful minority. Those who pay their subscriptions and contribute towards the future and security of their sport are fighting the battle for those who sit back and do nothing.

I would stress that the Association in no way offers shooting for its members; that would be an impossibility. However, the benefits are substantial. Individual members are covered for third party liability risks to the value of £1,000,000 in respect of any one accident. Nowhere else would one be able to buy a million pounds' worth of insurance for a tenner and in addition receive all the other benefits which the Association has to offer, including a glossy quarterly magazine which keeps one well informed on every aspect of shooting.

Shooting today requires accurate information, and of prime importance is the collection and assessment of information on all aspects of sporting shooting, especially its direct impact upon wildlife and the environment. Long-term studies, providing factual information on shooting, form part of

17

the Association's work, while studies on immediate issues are undertaken as necessary.

Wildlife populations are increasingly having to be managed at national and international levels, especially where, as in the case of migratory species, they are an internationally shared resource. The BASC works closely with national and international conservation and sporting bodies to promote the future of quarry species and their habitat. There are many areas where shooting takes place over sites of recognised ecological importance. Frequently these are influenced or controlled by BASC members whose shooting interest is traditional and long-standing. In every case the BASC seeks to survey and assess the sites for their nature conservation value, and to draw up management plans with conservation organisations, official bodies and local authorities as appropriate. The BASC affiliated clubs are encouraged and assisted in the acquisition of shooting leases so that the sensitive and scientifically important habitats can be managed fairly and sensibly for the benefit of all.

It is well worth while applying for membership of a local wildfowling or gun club. Often the membership list is an extensive one and you may have to wait your turn to be admitted. Provided that the club is affiliated to the BASC you will automatically qualify for all the benefits of an individual member by joining, and in some cases the club may actually lease its own shooting rights over which you will be able to shoot, depending upon club rules and regulations. You cannot afford to ignore the Association.

A beginner joining BASC will be able to learn all about his chosen sport far better than following a lone course. Through its active education programmes the BASC promotes basic levels of proficiency and sportsmanship, and through its publications the shooting public are kept well informed. Courses are held in gundog training, gamekeeping, wildfowling, shoot management, and other information is readily available. If you have a problem then the staff at Marford Mill will be only to happy to give advice.

The BASC *Codes of Practice* sets clear standards of acceptable sporting practice for rough-shooters, wildfowlers, air rifle sporting shooters and gamekeepers.

The Proficiency Award Scheme provides newcomers to the sport with a practical method of achieving self-confidence through a course of instruction and assessment, and to implement prescribed minimum standards of conduct in safety, sportsmanship and courtesy. The scheme is complemented by the Association's own *Handbook of Shooting – The Sporting Shotgun*.

There is also a Land Agency service in which BASC offers advice and practical assistance both to individual members and to affiliated clubs engaged in the acquisition of sporting rights. The Association's full-time Land Agent also provides advice to landowners wishing to realise the very real economic value of their sporting rights. As well as matching those with shooting to offer to those seeking sporting opportunities, guidance is given on capital and rental values, tenancy agreements and management policies. Equally, advice and information is provided to institutional landowners over all matters relating to the sport of shooting.

The Members' Shoot Advisory Service will give experienced advice so that many shoots, large or small, can be made to return a substantially improved quality of sport.

Careful and judicious tree planting, the correct distribution of game cover crops, the maintenance and management of ponds and lakes all assist in achieving the full potential of a shoot. The BASC can make recommendations on the most practical and suitable methods of pest control and the supplementing of wild game populations through restocking.

The legislation covering sporting shooting is complex, some laws dating back many years, a host of new ones introduced in the Wildlife and Countryside Act, 1981. Shooting legislation affects the sportsman in almost everything he does and through its Membership Advisory Service the Association ensures that members are kept up to date with every law and regulation which concerns their sport.

The Association has its own *Firearms Department*. It assists individual members with any problems concerned with gun ownership and looks after the interests of those who legitimately hold firearms for sporting purposes. Should there be any problems concerning obtaining a shotgun certificate or its renewal then you should contact the Association. Without their advice the beginner is at a disadvantage.

It is vital for the future of the sport, and for the future of our countryside, that the sportsman's voice is heard wherever decisions are taken, whether by parliament, local government, international agencies and other statutory or non-governmental organisations which affect the shooting man. The BASC provides that voice. At Westminster it operates through an all party *Parliamentary Committee* and maintains strong and active representation at every level. It is acknowledged and recognised by national and international agencies as a responsible and respected organisation. It provides factual information on matters affecting shooting, it presents the sportsman's case whenever and wherever it needs to be heard, and endeavours to correct any distorted information projected by those who may be opposed to the sport.

Above all, the BASC works for the future of sporting shooting and its place in the British countryside, in order that the sport can be handed down to our children and grandchildren in a healthy and flourishing condition.

You cannot do without the BASC.

The preliminaries are over; you are equipped, you are a BASC member. Now the search for somewhere to shoot can begin in earnest.

CHAPTER TWO

The Search for Shooting

The obvious place in which to begin the search for somewhere to shoot is in the classified advertisement columns of one of the shooting magazines. However, this should be carried out as early as possible *on the day of publication*, for if there is some shooting up for grabs then rest assured there will be a stampede for it.

You are interested in a rent which you can afford, an acreage of between 100 and 200 (although in a later chapter we shall look at 'pocket-handkerchief' shoots) and the quality of the land up for rent. 'Rough shooting' can mean anything from mixed farmland to barren grazing land. The fact that there may be little in the way of game on it at the time is immaterial; it can always be developed providing the *potential* is there. A couple of hundred acres of sheep farm where the stock have grazed the grass down to the butt and the hedges have been flail-cut to nothing is useless. Ideally the prospective tenant must look for somewhere with at least four or five acres of woodland, a patch of water (even the smallest pond is capable of being built-up into a duck shoot), and hopefully some root crops at the beginning of the season, either swedes, kale or rape to hold a few birds.

Market garden land is not generally conducive to good sport, mainly because the farmer has to be commercial and cannot afford to 'waste' land by allowing it to remain uneconomic. Hedges are no good to him, they shade the crops and generally he will have little in the way of livestock to contain by hedging so all he needs is a perimeter wire fence to safeguard his crops from other people's stock. The law is that a farmer must fence against his own stock and if a neighbour's sheep or cattle trespass then the owner is liable. No farmer is going to go to a lot of expense growing hedges for the benefit of a neighbour.

On market gardens there is usually a workforce in the fields most days which will disturb any game. Vegetables have to be marketed as fresh as possible and therefore any cover will have the maximum amount of disturbance. Carrots, cabbages, etc., do not provide a lot in the way of food for pheasants, only cover. All that this type of farming can really offer is

Try to rent some farmland adjoining your Forestry Commission shoot.
(Photo: Lance Smith)

pigeon-shooting during hard weather when the birds are desperate for anything edible. Treat the market garden as a good source for pigeons during December to February when the farmer may well be glad of your services. It is not worth paying a rent just for this.

Exploitation

One has to be wary of any shooting that is advertised. Unfortunately shooting, like many other sports, has become commercialised and this has added to the problems of the man of modest means. Affluence in agriculture has meant that the small farmer is no longer grateful for a few pounds in return for the sporting rights. Twenty years ago the average rental for rough shooting was in the region of 10s an acre. Nowadays it can be anything from £2 upwards, and if the landowner prices himself out of the market then he is not unduly worried; far better to have no shooting at all on his land than to let it for a nominal sum.

Then somebody came up with the idea of making even more money out of the aspiring rough-shooter – let shooting by the day, make a quick kill and save yourself the inconvenience of having a regular tenant who is likely to turn up at any time. So pigeon shooting was advertised at £5 to £10 a day. The response was overwhelming so greedy landowners decided that they had

21

underpriced their commodity and began asking £15 to £20. In some cases the asking price is £30, accommodation and food extra. But what do you get for your money?

It all depends. A farmer with little interest in shooting who has noticed a few woodpigeons flying about his land is under the impression that anybody with a gun and a few decoys will make a sizeable bag. What he does not realise is that pigeons might be feeding on his farm one day and be three farms away the next. So if you don't get a shot that's your bad luck! Woodlands may offer some roost-shooting but only for a couple of hours in the late afternoon and evening so you could be paying up to £15 an hour to fire a dozen shots, and if the wood is overshot the birds will soon go somewhere else.

If in desperation you decide to take a day's pigeon-shooting on these terms then go and call on the farmer, listen to what he has to say and insist on a day's reconnaissance, without a gun, beforehand. If he is not agreeable to that then he knows full well that there is little to offer in the way of sport.

Where rough-shooting is offered, you expect to find a pheasant or two, plus rabbits and pigeons. Any landowner selling shooting this way should be prepared to rear and release a few pheasants; he might get away with wild birds for the first day or two but after that he will have a barren acreage and is, in effect, taking your money under false pretences.

'Rough-shooting' can mean anything from barren grazing land to mixed farmland. (Photo: Lance Smith)

Approaching farmers

Let us assume that your efforts with the classified advertisements have drawn a blank. You have phoned about two possibilities but the sporting has already been let; there is a third but the travelling distance is too great. Shoots too far from home can present a variety of problems. I drove a regular round-trip of 140 miles each week to my present shoot before I finally moved to live on it, and in the winter months such journeys can be both exhausting and treacherous. They can mar the enjoyment of an otherwise successful day. Also there are difficulties where pheasants are released; you are not on the spot to feed regularly, you cannot trap vermin because you are not on hand to inspect your traps daily, and if poachers decide to raid you they will go unhindered. The alternative is to enlist the help of a reliable part-time keeper but even so I think one's shoot should be no more than fifty miles from home.

The personal approach to farmers is undoubtedly the best method. However, some forethought is advisable before setting out on such a quest. Let us for the moment put ourselves in the farmer's position.

Country folk are by nature, and rightly so, suspicious people. For generations they have been left unmolested to go about their rural activities and then an affluent society with the means of transport brought them into contact with townspeople. A few irresponsibles created a bad image that will take a long time to die; trespassing picnickers left gates open and livestock got out, motorised poachers toured the quiet lanes early on Sunday mornings looking for a quick shot at an unsuspecting pheasant over the hedge. The car-rallies arrived with their after-dark noise and nuisance. And as a result the town-dweller's image was tarnished. The sportsman has the task of convincing the farmer that he is honest and reliable, that he understands the ways of the countryside. It isn't easy.

Why should a farmer let his shooting rights? If it is for money then the asking price will be high to make it worth his while. Yet there are reasons other than financial why he should agree to have a sporting tenant walking his fields.

Farmers who do not shoot for sport are inclined to be wary of having others with guns on their land. In effect, letting the shooting rights is parting with some of the farmer's independence. An outsider has been given the *right* to carry a gun on the farm. Often farmers 'barter' shooting in exchange for casual labour at harvest time. It is the carrot which will persuade the young man from the village to come and load up a few bales, but if general permission to shoot is given to several locals it can become a nuisance. The farmer therefore needs a ready and convincing excuse to say 'sorry, I'm afraid I can't let you shoot here and that goes for anybody else' – and the best excuse is *because the shooting is let to a reliable outsider*. It saves him the constant embarrassment of trying to deter locals from continually pestering him for shooting. And *you* could be the ready means to this end.

First consult an ordnance survey map of the area you wish to explore; you will stand more chance in places away from the towns for those will surely have already been snapped up and will probably be poached as well.

A Sunday is not a good day for your foray. Farmers will be doubly suspicious of callers on the sabbath so take a weekday off from work and approach the business systematically. Dress is important; don't go in your shooting clothes as though you expect to start shooting right away. It is presumptuous. Likewise a city suit gives the wrong impression and looks out of place in rural areas. Strike a happy medium, casually but smartly dressed, perhaps a sports jacket and flannels, and a BASC badge on your car *might* just convince a farmer that you care about your sport.

It is inadvisable for more than two of you to make the initial approach. A carload of hopeful sportsmen can give the impression that a gang of trigger-happy shooters are waiting to descend on the rural scene. Farmers are more likely to rent or give permission to the loner, or the one who brings a companion, than to a 'syndicate'.

Study the terrain carefully before you begin knocking on doors. Steep hillsides which are mostly grazing land with a few stunted thorn bushes and patches of gorse are unlikely to offer much in the way of sport if you are successful in obtaining the rights. What you are looking for is the small farm with some woodland on it and perhaps a pool or a stream.

Village pubs are almost invariably the source of such information but, once again, the approach has to be subtle. Don't give the immediate impression to the landlord that you are out on an expedition to find shooting because he will probably spread the word that evening as a kind of 'warning' to his customers. It might also prompt a few of the casual shooters to get in first.

Bring up the subject of shooting casually during the course of conversation, enquire who shoots that big wood down the road. Perhaps the landlord will tell you that so-and-so shoots that right up to Farmer Jones's boundary. And who shoots Farmer Jones's land? Well, his son used to but he's got married and got a farm of his own now and the old man's getting past it. Your pulses begin to race but you must remain calm. Certainly Mr Jones is worth a visit.

Now you must choose your time carefully. Nobody, farmer or otherwise, likes to be disturbed in the middle of a meal. And farmers often go straight back out to the fields as soon as they have eaten. Countryfolk traditionally usually lunch around 1 pm so a good time to arrive would be about 1.30. Don't drive right into the farmyard, again it looks presumptuous. Park your vehicle close to the entrance, but not blocking it, and approach the house on foot.

There is no point in beating about the bush now. If you go into a long

A rough corner on an otherwise neat commercial farm. (Photo: Lance Smith)

preamble about the weather Farmer Jones's suspicions will at once be aroused. False humility will go against you as will an air of arrogance. Simply tell him that you are looking for a shoot and you wondered if he might be interested, or if not perhaps he knows of another farmer who might be.

Do not expect an immediate response. Unless of course the answer is in the negative, as it surely will be on some occasions. If he asks you in for a cup of tea then at least he has not totally thrown out the idea but he will obviously want to know more about you first. In some instances it is helpful to take a wife or girlfriend along with you. Farmers' wives, who spend most of their time around the precincts of the farm, are often glad of the opportunity of female company and there have been instances where the sportsman's spouse has been instrumental in winning the day for him!

Naturally the farmer will want to know who you are and where you come from. Don't make the mistake of pushing the issue too hard. If he seems undecided that is because for him it is a major decision. Is he to allow this total stranger to roam his land with a gun?

You may come away perplexed, not knowing whether you are going to get the shooting or not. He may need time to make his mind up, talk it over with his wife. Or he may opt for a middle course – 'Come down next weekend and have a shot, see how you get on.' Which means he is putting you on trial before committing himself which is only fair.

Let us assume that after much fruitless searching you have at last found a Farmer Jones who has agreed to let you the shooting of his 150-acre farm. The hardest part is over but now you need to tie up the details to the satisfaction of both parties.

Some farmers do not like signing written agreements. To attempt to press one into doing so might result in the loss of the shoot and all the hard groundwork which has gone before. If your new landlord is against the idea then try to settle on a gentleman's agreement but go over all the points very carefully with him. The main items to establish are:

1. Do you have the *sole* shooting rights or is this just permission to shoot and other casual shots will be allowed on the land?

2. Are you entitled to all the rabbits, including taking by nets with ferrets? Sometimes the rabbiting is let separately.

3. Can you shoot whenever you wish and bring other guns with you?

The issue of rent is negotiable. Pay by cheque whenever possible as this constitutes a receipt, and if the farmer is unwilling to sign an agreement he will probably resist giving you a receipt. *But you must have some proof of your rights.* I quote a case involving a friend of mine. He had rented a particular acreage previously and renewed it again on 2 February, the date from which shoots are officially let. Some time later, whilst out for a stroll round with his gun, he encountered another irate shooter who accused him of poaching. What had actually happened was that the farmer had let the shoot *twice*, trusting to luck that neither 'tenant' would meet up with the other!

So many private shoots are let in good faith and only a minority run into troubled waters. Various arrangements may be made but I am unhappy with any that involve anything other than a straight cash payment. Once, many years ago, I rented 100 acres of meadowland for £5 a year but the additional proviso was that the farmer had half the birds I shot. I had no objection to this at the time; if I shot a brace of birds, he had one. If I only killed a single bird I gave it to him. But it all fell apart one freezing January night at the commencement of that bitter winter of 1962/63.

A stretch of river bordered the lower part of the shoot, and I had invited three friends to flight duck with me. As dusk fell we crouched at strategic intervals along the bank and suddenly the teal began to flight. I have never known a teal flight like that one before or since. Birds hurtled at us in the failing light in twos and threes incessantly, and we were firing and reloading as fast as our numbed fingers would allow. Remus, my yellow labrador, seemed impervious to the icy water as he retrieved teal after teal.

Darkness came and still the ducks were coming. All four of us had shot out of cartridges for a total bag of a dozen teal. We returned to the car, opened the door by heating the lock with a cigarette lighter to unfreeze it, and drove back to the farm. And ten minutes later an obviously suspicious farmer's wife regarded the teal laid out for her.

'Is that all you've got?' she stared in genuine disbelief. 'You've been shooting all evening, you must've got a bagful of *proper* ducks, not those little 'uns! Those aren't worth the trouble of plucking!'

So a night of superb sport ended with an anti-climax.

One factor that *might* just sway a farmer into letting you shoot on his land is your BASC indemnity against shooting accidents. But on no account use the name of the Association as a lever. There have been cases in the past where members who have trespassed, either deliberately or in ignorance, have produced their membership cards when accosted and tried to bluff land-owners that it entitles them to shoot where they want. Such an action would undoubtedly result in expulsion from the BASC.

Poachers

This is a tricky subject where private landowners are concerned and it is best to discuss it with the farmer before an instance actually arises. Farmers know everybody in the locality and if you catch a local poaching the farmer will probably not want a court case. On the other hand, leniency can often lead to further poaching. I have run into this problem more than once on my various shoots in the past. All too often the 'moocher' is brazen, the old story about 'old Jack's always let me shoot here and I'm not going to stop now'.

There are a number of subtle ways of putting a stop to this. He may well hold a shotgun certificate but it's odds on that he hasn't got a game licence. The farmer won't openly condone these nefarious activities but likewise he will not do anything positive about it. If your poacher has shot game then let him know that you intend to ask the police to check on his game licence.

We shall deal more in detail with serious poachers, however, in a later chapter. Likewise, now that you have acquired your own little rough shoot we shall discuss ways in which it may be improved and built-up to yield a return for your trouble and cash outlay.

The lucky one has found his shoot but there will be others frustrated by their efforts, despairing of ever finding anywhere. Their outings have proved fruitless, farmhouse doors have been slammed in their faces even though their approach has been right. They have gone back to the advertisement columns of their favourite sporting magazine, have even advertised for a small rough shoot and received not a single reply.

And then, suddenly, they spot an inch-square advertisement which virtually screams out at them. It may read like this:

'Sporting rights over 500 hectares on . . . Tenders by . . . Details from Forestry Commission . . .'

Truly the Forestry Commission have put many thousands of acres of shooting within reach of the average shooter, whereas years ago this land was privately owned and often part of large estates. This type of shooting has both advantages and disadvantages and these we shall look at in the next chapter.

CHAPTER THREE

Forestry Commission Shoots

Perhaps the best way to illustrate a typical Forestry Commission shoot is to describe how I came by my own shoot nearly twenty-five years ago and which now adjoins my own smallholding.

One dismal September day in 1963 a shooting companion and myself motored seventy miles to inspect the Black Hill which is an afforested hill 1,400 feet above sea level on the Shropshire/Welsh border. At the time I was also renting 180 acres of Economic Forestry woodland adjoining my own garden, plus 200 acres of arable and two flight ponds within six miles of my home. Why, indeed, was I searching for shooting so far away?

This convenient wood was scheduled for felling and there were rumours that the land might be quarried. Also, the rent was nominal and the owners would not lease it for longer than a year-to-year basis which gave me the feeling that it was only temporary. As for the farmland, the farmer was nearing retirement and was only a tenant anyway, so I could see this arrangement being terminated in the near future. I decided to find other pastures whilst there was time instead of having to search frantically for somewhere to shoot.

But I came to the Black Hill by accident. Initially I tendered for a small Forestry Commission shoot nearer to home but the project was fated. This was land recently acquired by the Commission, and during the early part of the summer I went and walked the ground over and submitted an offer which seemed to be acceptable. Then weeks went by and I heard nothing. It transpired that the former owner had not realised when he sold the land that he was parting with the shooting rights and on hearing of my tour of inspection he at once contacted the Forestry Commission. The latter generally favour a former owner in such a case and this belated request was given priority over my offer. Consequently, with some embarrassment, they informed me that they were unable to lease me the sporting of this small shoot but informed me that there was a 500-acre forest on the Shropshire/Welsh border which I could have for a nominal rent.

It appeared that nobody wanted the shooting on the Black Hill; it had not

A typical Forestry Commission shoot. (Photo: Lance Smith)

been leased since the days when it formed part of the Cwm Estate, halcyon days when there were grouse and blackgame amongst the heather slopes and only the odd scrub tree. A barren backwater in the early sixties, the grouse gone along with the heather and in their place row after row of symmetrical conifer saplings where one had to walk across deep-ploughed furrows.

The hill was enshrouded in a thick mist that day and I did not see much of it. Grassy rides and fire-breaks led up to the summit and my companion and I wondered what the view was like beyond. I decided to take a chance and offered an annual rent of £20 for three years. After all, this was only a stop-gap and in the meantime I could view other Forestry shoots and maybe find somewhere better and nearer home. The ultimate result was that at the end of the three years I renewed the lease for a further seven years and up until the present day have had a series of five-year leases. I bought a smallholding on the hill itself and moved to live here. Not, I stress, that the shoot was ever an exceptional one; but the place with its panoramic views and extremes in weather conditions had an appeal that went deeper than any abundance of game could ever have done with me.

Those early years were certainly barren ones. There were few pigeons because the trees had not yet grown to roosting height, and the rabbit population had been decimated by several outbreaks of myxomatosis. The only species in abundance were corvines, foxes and grey squirrels. That first season I killed twenty-eight foxes, mostly cubs; I did not shoot a pheasant until the second year, indeed that old cock bird was the first I saw and he had certainly been on the hill much longer than I had!

There was a small natural pool in the heart of the big wood, so clear that you could drink from it on a hot day. I fed it hopefully but for weeks that barley lay untouched in the shallows. Then one day, having given up all hope of seeing wild duck at this height, I approached the pool without stealth and flushed a number of mallard. More by luck than marksmanship I dropped a couple and from that day onwards duck have always flighted into that little pond. I am inclined to think that the disturbance of planting had disturbed them for a year or two and once everywhere resumed an atmosphere of normality they returned.

Rearing pheasants was quite out of the question in those early years. My entire terrain consisted of conifer thickets and vermin, and if I was to build up a stock of pheasants then I had somehow to acquire the shooting rights of some of the farmland adjoining the forest.

This took time. I was virtually in the position of the town-dweller who sets forth to find some shooting in unknown territory. Naturally I was regarded with suspicion by some of the neighbouring farmers who today are close friends of mine. I was the chap who arrived at weekends to 'bang away in the forest'. I could not possibly be up to any good!

Slowly that situation changed. I did not try to rush it; indeed I never mentioned my interest in any adjacent shooting and I took good care not to trespass on any of the farmland. But it was my constant war on the foxes that provided my big breakthrough. Hill-farmers hate foxes, for Reynard will plunder their lambing fields unmercifully during the spring of the year and their poultry houses are always in danger.

In those days vermin-gibbets were a common sight where any keepering was carried out. The hanging corpses were proof of a keeper's efficiency. So I began to display my own kills. One farmer kept a count of the foxes I hung up with great enthusiasm and before long he extended an invitation to me to walk his own steep hillsides. There was no mention of game and I did not take advantage of the situation. Then, the following autumn, he remarked that there was a cock pheasant in his five acres of rape most days and 'if you go quietly you'm sure to get 'im.' I did, and the following year I broached the question of releasing a few birds.

The farmer in question was full of enthusiasm, and even found me a broody hen. The exercise was only partly successful and those first dozen poults strayed elsewhere but, nevertheless, the foundation had been laid for a regular rearing programme. No rent was asked or offered, to have done so would, I feel, have been an insult to this son of the hills. A few small presents at Christmas for his family ensured that I had all the shooting I wanted on his small farm.

A year or two later I was successful in renting the next farm for £5 a year. By now there were a few pheasants to be found in the locality. I well remember bringing my father down to shoot one day and although we set out from home on a bright sunny morning, the further west we travelled the more the weather worsened. By the time we arrived at the hill the rain was torrential and we sat in the car for half an hour trying to decide what we were going to do; it was only too clear from the sky that the rain had set in for the day.

In the end we decided to brave the elements for an hour, beat through the rape and the swedes and then call it a day. Ironically, that hour will remain in my memory for many years to come and just goes to show how unpredictable the sport of shooting can be. It seemed that every pheasant on the hill was in the roots that morning when you would have expected them to be sheltering in the depths of the forest. We each had a right and left and finished up with a bag which would have been exceptional for a full day's shooting in the hills on a day when conditions favoured the sportsman.

Shoots come and go, but I am a firm believer that when one door closes, another opens. Both these farms changed hands and I lost the shooting but I was fortunate in renting another couple, together with twenty-seven acres of surprisingly flat and boggy land within a hundred yards of my present home on the hill. This latter is a good inland snipe marsh and draws a few duck as well. By shooting sparingly one can have regular sport throughout the season.

But I would stress that it took me fifteen years to establish the shooting which I now have, the focal point being the big Forestry Commission wood which in the beginning had little to offer in the way of sport; but by a gradual process my present shoot was built up. One must be patient, be content with whatever is on offer when there is nothing else available, and assess the potential.

Let us now take a look at Forestry Commission shoots in general and what they have to offer.

The Forestry Commission's policy

The Forestry Commission was formed in 1919. An afforestation programme was necessary, the war had taken its toll of our timber and with the advent of commercial farming many private woodlands were to disappear over the next fifty years.

The majority of the Commission's land covers terrain which is unsuitable for anything other than sheep grazing. Land was put to good use, the only drawback being the disappearance of vast tracts of heather on which the grouse survived. As a result grouse and blackgame numbers declined. My own shoot, the Black Hill, once was the habitat of grouse and blackgame but sadly these birds are to be seen no longer here. Much of this land was sold very cheaply to the Forestry Commission; I note from my own deeds that the twenty-seven acres adjoining my smallholding was purchased by the Commission for £100!

However, jobs have been created in remote rural areas where otherwise there would be none, and Britain's afforestation has been made economically viable. Nowadays more forethought is given to planting and re-planting and often areas of hardwood break up the monotony of a coniferous landscape.

But this is only one of the Forestry Commission's functions. Many woodlands are open to the public for recreation purposes, picnic sites have been introduced, together with a conservation programme, and this is a matter upon which the prospective shooting tenant must co-operate with his landlords.

Over half the Commission's land has either been leased to former owners or reserved by agreement at the time of the sale. Other areas are not let because shooting would conflict with the recreational activities and would damage press and public relations. A remaining percentage of forestry land has been designated as Sites of Special Scientific Interest (SSSI) and we shall look at these, together with the Wildlife and Countryside Act 1981, in the chapter on overall conservation.

Where sporting is available for letting it is done so by competitive tender, on a three or five year lease. The land in question is offered in the press and those interested are invited to send for details. They may then go and inspect the area; forestry rangers are usually most helpful in arranging this. After that, the onus is on the sportsman to submit an offer.

Determining a rent

There is no hard and fast rule to rental value of forestry shooting. Newly acquired land that has yet to be planted is of greater value than an existing mature wood where there is little in the way of food for game. A forest usually offers good sport for the first few years after planting but as the trees mature the shooting potential declines. This is something which has to be taken into consideration when making an offer; right now the land looks good, there is plenty of cover that is conducive to game but what will it be like in ten years time? Bear in mind that once the plantations reach maturity, in say twenty-five years' time, they may not be felled automatically even then. Supply and demand will be an instrumental factor where timber is concerned just like any other product, and who can forecast a quarter of a century ahead? Foreign suppliers may be dominating the market and trees will not be felled just for the sake of it. They will be harvested when there is a definite market.

Felling has just commenced on my own forestry shoot. For the last five years the plantations have been impenetrable to all except my spaniel and my sport has been restricted to the forestry roads. The flight pond has become overshadowed by tall pines so that the duck have difficulty in seeing the water at deep dusk. Wild duck like cover round a pond but they do not like trees which obstruct their departure in an emergency. Likewise, the dense undergrowth obstructs vision and on occasions when I have flushed a mallard off the water I have been unable to get a shot at it.

Most forestry shoots have water in some form on them, whether it is a natural pool or an artificial reservoir for fire-fighting purposes. The latter are not much good, symmetrical and deep; duck like shallow water in which they can dabble, and some reeds for cover.

Inspect your Forestry Commission shoot *thoroughly* before making an offer and take various factors into consideration. How long has it been planted and approximately when will it be felled? If there is a pool look for signs of duck using it, the odd preening feather, tracks through the algae where the birds have swum and fed. *But even if there are no signs remember that duck can always be encouraged to use the pool with the right management.*

Pay particular attention to your boundaries and enquire who your neighbours are and whether they shoot. The perimeter of an established wood offers the best potential for that is where pheasants will be found. The birds will use the thick trees for roosting but with the coming of daylight they will head for the fields in search of food. Unless you can rent some of the adjoining land there is little point in embarking upon a rearing programme for all you will be doing is providing somebody else with sport. In some cases you may well have to accept that a Forestry Commission shoot will provide you only with rabbits and pigeon.

Yet there is always the unexpected factor to be taken into account. Even if you have settled for a rough vermin shoot there are those occasions when you will flush a pheasant in the most unlikely place. And don't forget woodcock; these superlative sporting birds usually arrive in Britain at the beginning of November and are found in most woodlands, particularly shortly after their migratory flight. I remember one day when a companion and myself flushed no fewer than sixteen from a thick patch of larch. We did not see another woodcock for the rest of the season. Newly arrived birds had found somewhere to rest up and once they were refreshed they departed in search of a more suitable habitat. All the same, there are very few seasons when I don't shoot a woodcock in these woods.

The governing factors in any Forestry Commission sporting tenders are acreage and potential. Rents vary throughout the country from as little as 50p an acre in upland areas to a much higher rent for lowland territory in 'shooting country'. Bear in mind that the shooting rights will go to the highest bidder, you don't get a second chance, so you need to make a realistic offer and determine what the value is to yourself. Unfortunately the value of sporting can be grossly inflated where a prospective syndicate is prepared to

A woodcock in the bag; these birds arrive in Britain at the beginning of November. (Photo: Calvin Williams)

offer a high price just for the right to carry a gun on land, irrespective of whether it has potential. All too often the genuine novice who would have been prepared to build up a neglected shoot is outbid.

Go and look at the area. Then, on your return home, sit down with a pencil and paper and do some 'costing'. Acreage, forestry management and felling schedule must all be taken into consideration as also must the distance of your proposed shoot from your home. Work out *your* expenses, including rearing and releasing a few birds and weigh it up against how much *you* can afford. You cannot do more than that; make your offer, don't be too optimistic, and in the meantime continue your search for shooting.

If you are the lucky one then in due course the Forestry Commission will contact you and you will be offered a lease. But before you sign this and accept new responsibilities it is as well that we take a brief look at some of the main clauses in a Forestry Commission lease.

Sporting leases

The landlord (Forestry Commission) lets *all* the exclusive right of sporting by shooting and the taking away of birds and animals as follows: teal, mallard, grouse, partridge, pheasant, pigeon, snipe, woodcock, hares and rabbits.

On my current lease blackgame, wild fowl and capercaillie have been deleted to be replaced by 'mallard and teal'. I am most unlikely to come across any of the former three species with the exception of mallard and teal but obviously this has been altered on the remote chance of any of them deciding to use my shoot as a habitat.

The landlord retains the right to kill or authorise others to kill 'any bird or animal which he or his agent considers may become a source of injury to any woods, plantations, crops, or pastures belonging to the landlord, his tenants or adjoining occupiers'. The tenant is also *obliged* to control the various species as follows: crows, gulls, jays, magpies, pigeons, rats, foxes, grey squirrels, hares, stoats, weasels, rabbits, mink and coypu.

In many areas the forestry rangers wage constant war on grey squirrels and rabbits which are the main enemies of afforestation. Grey squirrels are controlled by warfarin bait laid in tunnels, and where rabbits present a threat to young trees they are usually controlled by gassing. It is important to get to know your local forestry rangers and work in conjunction with them. We are all conservationists and vermin species must be controlled for the sake of wildlife in general.

The landlord is entitled to give permission to the local Hunt to draw the woods but the Hunt should, out of courtesy, advise you of any dates when they may be hunting in your woods. It is only good manners. Failure to do this on their part may result in a day's shooting being spoiled or, worse, hounds running into fox-snares which you have set and are inspecting daily in compliance with the Wildlife and Countryside Act 1981.

The landlord has the right to allow the public access to woods for the 'purpose of air and exercise'. This is something which the tenant must accept and, indeed, in no way should it be detrimental to sport. It means that you must be safety conscious at all times and never shoot where you cannot see. Access can be interpreted as walking on forestry roads, not rampaging through the plantations. Dogs must be kept under control and if you come across anybody with an unruly dog then it is your duty to remonstrate with them. In the case of any unreasonable behaviour by members of the public the Commission will be glad of your support.

You are required to pay the rent on time, usually on 2 February. Delayed payments may result in problems with the renewal of your lease when it becomes due.

You must consult your local Forestry Commission office before erecting any release pens. The important thing is not to take liberties, to build up a good relationship with local officers and most reasonable requests will be granted. Look upon yourself as gamekeeper/custodian of the woodlands and the environment. Forestry rangers have vast tracts of land to patrol and they will be grateful for any assistance.

You are required to maintain an insurance policy indemnifying the landlord up to £250,000, in respect of any one claim in the event of a shooting accident. Your BASC membership will take care of this for four times that amount, and you are likewise obliged to ascertain that any who shoot with you are also suitably insured.

Leases may vary from area to area, and be up-dated periodically as new legislation is introduced, so you must understand fully the responsibilities you are taking on. Some of the clauses may sound awe-inspiring to the beginner but in effect they are just common sense. This is no willy-nilly agreement for you to carry a gun on land; you are a tenant of the Forestry Commission and as such you have certain rights which you may not have on a privately negotiated shoot.

Deer

You are not entitled to shoot deer on your Forestry Commission shoot. Indeed, it is illegal to kill them with shotguns except in special circumstances using heavy buckshot and, anyway, this is not a book for the stalker. The Commission organise stalking by the day in certain areas and those wishing to know more about this should contact the Forestry Commission.

On balance I believe that Forestry Commission shoots are good value for money if your expectations are not too high. What you make of the shoot is up to you and if all you want is some sport with pigeons and rabbits then most shoots will offer this in some degree.

My own reaction after my first season was one of immense relief. The pressure was not on me to kill birds so that a farmer landlord could have a brace, and I was left strictly to my own plans; I could shoot when I wanted, there was complete privacy and I was actually the boss of the shoot. I would wholeheartedly recommend the aspiring novice to try one of these shoots for an initial three-year period. If at the end of that time you don't think it is your scene then the agreement can be terminated without the embarrassment of explaining to a friendly farmer that you don't think his shoot is any good and you don't want to rent it any longer.

Renewing a lease is generally no problem. An existing tenant will be given priority over other shoot-hunters and one does not have to go through the whole business of tendering for the shoot again. Usually an increased rent is asked but this is negotiable and if you have genuine reasons for believing that this is not warranted then you have the opportunity to state your case.

In some instances shooting may be withdrawn from certain forestry acreages but this is usually because other recreational activities are not in harmony with shotgun sport. Whatever the problems, meet them as they arise and in the meantime build up your shoot and enjoy your sport.

CHAPTER FOUR

The Small Rough Shoot

My interest in shooting began at the age of seven on a rough shoot of ninety acres, farmland which was surely the textbook example of what a rough shoot should comprise. It was within half a mile of my home and on Saturday afternoons, from September through to the beginning of March, I used to accompany my father on his weekly forays.

There were two woods, the New Plantation wood of some twenty acres, mostly silver birch and rhododendrons, ideal woodcock terrain. The other, known as The Hanging Wood (where Cromwell was reputed to have hanged 100 Royalists) consisted of mature oaks and beech and always held a pheasant or two.

Then there was a rather odd five acres of seeded, ungrazed grassland, bordering a disused quarry, which always harboured a covey of partridge. This was our starting point each week; a covey whirring up, heading back towards the quarry.

I will always remember the potato field. I have firmly fixed in my memory a recollection of the ageing tenant farmer and his wife harvesting their crop, he digging the tubers up with a fork whilst she loaded them into hessian sacks!

The farm was untidy, the crops were poor. There always seemed to be odd patches of unharvested corn and the knee-high stubble often remained until ploughing time in the spring. Sadly there was no water but I remember once my father shot a mallard in the oak wood as it quacked up from a carpet of acorns.

There were rabbits in abundance and we seldom returned home with less than ten. Food rationing was still in force and I know that my father used to take a proportion of our bag to needy households on the following Monday morning. Woodcock were usually destined for the bishop's palace because the holy man had a liking for them. I remember, too, the day the bishop came shooting with us and some unfortunate farm labourers, lunching behind a hedge, were lucky to escape a charge of shot fired hastily at a departing low-flying covey of birds by a careless prebendary. There was an enraged roar

This overgrown quarry might hold the odd rabbit. (Photo: Lance Smith)

from these men but it was my father who smoothed the matter over and the luckless (or lucky!) workers were on the point of going and apologising to the bishop for their colourful expletives!

Those were the days, when game was plentiful and life was just that pace slower, when my father shot with crimson-cased Maximum cartridges loaded with Neoflak powder, or sometimes used the green Remington Shurshot with corrugated shells; when hedgerows were several feet thick and the dog bolted rabbits with consistent regularity, and I learned to swing after them with an unloaded .410 that had been confiscated from a local 'moocher'. These youthful memories I have attempted to resurrect on my own smallholding, an island in the midst of a sea of modern farming policies that are destructive to wildlife and a once-natural habitat.

Yet all is not lost. We have to move with the times but some of that former sporting scene can be rescued with the right management.

Let us go back to that enthusiast who has successfully persuaded Farmer Jones to lease the shooting of his small farm. The farmer has consented because he now has a handy excuse to tell those youths in the village that they cannot shoot over his land any longer. Your 'face fits' and your wife gets on well with his wife. The first hurdle is cleared, now you have to build up a much-neglected shoot.

The land is a mixture of modern farming techniques and a sprinkling of untidiness that one might expect from a farmer who is getting on in years. Two ten-acre woods that are fenced off from the livestock and, apart from the felling of a few odd trees for the farmhouse firewood supply for the winter, are left undisturbed. That is fine except that it is becoming too overgrown in places, and a day's work with a billhook would soon open up those rides again. All woods should have sunny places where pheasants can scratch around after acorns in the warmth of a late October day. These birds do not favour damp gloomy woods; a few small clearings amidst the dense briars and bracken will go a long way towards enhancing the sporting potential. Likewise, cover that is too thick does not make for good shooting; either the pheasants will hear you crashing your way through the bracken and move off long before you are within shot, or else you will have difficulty in getting a clear shot at any bird that rises.

Look at the woodland objectively and decide how you can tidy it up a bit. You will also need clearings in which to feed your birds because once the acorns and beechmast are finished, unless there is an alternative supply of food, the game will move on in search of a more acceptable habitat.

The job is not as awe-inspiring as it might at first appear. The main thing is to approach it with the right attitude. A couple of well-worn sayings spring to mind; nothing any good was ever done in a hurry, nor was Rome built in a day. And this is applicable to building up a shoot.

There is no point in rearing and releasing pheasants unless you have a habitat which will encourage them to stay at home. Pheasants are born wanderers and they take a lot of persuading to remain within the precincts of a small wood.

All you actually need to do is to make the wood light and airy and to ensure that there is ample food so that they do not need to go and search elsewhere for it, because once they have found an alternative they will not return.

Cut a main ride from one end of the wood to the other. Few woods are not dissected by a footpath of some kind so all you need to do is to open it up. One of the curses of most woods is the seeding down of silver birches which soon grow into sizeable saplings but short work can be made of these with a chainsaw. You will have to start sometime so better to create a disturbance when game is sparse than to drive off a batch of hand-reared birds.

Release-pens

You will not keep any pheasants at home without a suitable release-pen, and having thinned out your woodlands, begin work on this before you start trying to hatch any birds.

The purpose of a release-pen is to hold your pheasant poults in the wood at the time when they are most vulnerable to vermin and to give them time to settle and become acclimatised to their surroundings. *The pen must be their home*, they must recognise it as such and learn to return to it; it must be a fortress that is impenetrable to ground and winged vermin.

The basic structure will encompass anything from half an acre to an acre of your wood, depending upon how many birds you intend to rear, but the amateur is advised to begin with a modest programme and learn by experience. I favour strong galvanised 1-inch mesh, no less than 6 feet high and buried at least 6 inches in the ground in order to deter foxes from digging their way in underneath it. You will need 'funnels' at various points so that the birds can leave the pen to forage in the woods and return, but small enough to prevent entry by a fox. A friendly gamekeeper is best consulted on this point because if not securely made these exits and entrances could prove to be the weak link in an otherwise vermin-proof structure. Usually gamekeepers are most helpful and will advise those whom they see are making a positive effort to rear game; they are less likely to help the beginner who sees an easy way out by enticing neighbouring game on to his preserves.

You cannot be too thorough where foxes are concerned; you only need to have one find a way in and he will kill every pheasant in the enclosure. Renardine or creosote are excellent deterrents; soak every length of woodwork with either until the air reeks of this pungent stench. Suspend a few empty

Release-pen mesh must be buried at least 6 inches in the ground.
(Photo: Dave Cluett)

tin cans from surrounding branches with a drop of creosote in them to keep the smell strong.

Then, where possible, surround your pen with an electric fence. Your kindly farmer might even lend you his if it is not in current use, which it often is not during the summer months when sheep and cattle are usually not strip-grazing. With a live circuit, your wire buried deep enough in the ground and the atmosphere reeking of creosote/Renardine you ought not to have any problems with foxes. But there is still one very vulnerable, so far unprotected, area of your pen and that is the top.

Large release-pens in woods are often impracticable to roof and even nylon mesh would prove prohibitive from a cost point of view; erecting it would be near-impossible where you have trees growing inside the pen higher than the perimeter fence.

The main danger comes from birds of prey, particularly buzzards. And to make life even more difficult for the gamekeeper, these birds are protected by law. Up until fairly recently I never regarded the buzzard as a major threat, more a hunter like myself who takes the odd bird for his own consumption. This largest of our native hawks, with the exception of the golden eagle, will sit motionless for hours, perfectly camouflaged in a dead tree, until his prey emerges when he will drop down swiftly on it. But it is a different story when he discovers a concentration of pheasant poults which are accessible.

Only a few weeks ago at the time of writing, a shooting colleague of mine, a man of vast experience in the field, decided to build up a small rough shoot on the lines I have mentioned, and his first task was the construction of a release-pen. No detail was spared and the finished product was a veritable Fort Knox; no fox could have found a way inside. A batch of six-week-old pheasant poults were put in the pen. The following day my friend checked on them; there did not appear to be many inside the enclosure but as the area was large, and there was plenty of cover, he did not worry unduly. He refrained from going inside because he did not wish to alarm them.

The next morning he only counted six and decided that he had better investigate. There were, indeed, very few poults left in the release-pen and in places he came upon scattered feathers, but it was some time before he solved the mystery. A single buzzard had found the birds and was fetching them one by one. This bird of prey will take pheasant after pheasant, stacking them in an old nest, far more than it can eat.

If you cannot roof your release-pen against winged vermin then the best solution is an effigy. A life-sized one is easily made out of an old plastic sack stuffed with straw or newspapers. Dress it realistically with a hat and a gaudy hallowe'en mask, and drape it in a polythene coat that flaps continually in the wind. Move it every few days so that the predators do not become used to it and realise that it is only a dummy.

43

Vermin control

The control of vermin is something which needs to be undertaken before you commence rearing. February and March are the best months for a purge when the foliage is off the trees and you can spot the grey squirrel dreys easily. Poke them out, shoot any squirrels that bolt. Every one accounted for now will mean a litter less in a few weeks' time.

Tunnel-trapping is probably the most effective way of coming to terms with ground vermin. In order to save time when inspecting a relay of traps, tunnels constructed from three pieces of wood (two sides and a top) are more quickly lifted than having to dismantle ones built of stones or turf. Make sure that your trap is not restricted in any way and springs easily inside the tunnel.

Fenn humane vermin traps are reliable killers. Set them in your tunnels and cover them lightly with dead leaves or grass. There is no need to use bait

Traps should be sprung weekly if they have not caught. (Photo: Lance Smith)

because creatures such as grey squirrels, stoats, weasels, polecats, even rats, will travel through them provided they can see daylight at the other end. These inquisitive animals seem unable to resist exploring any tunnel they come across.

It is illegal to set any spring trap in the open. As a precaution against catching one of your pheasants by mistake it is a good idea to restrict both entrances to the tunnel with a couple of sticks stuck in the ground. Check your traps twice daily, first thing in the morning and last thing at night. If you have enough traps set you will soon reduce your vermin. The best places to site tunnel traps are by gateways or along a stone wall. Traps set haphazardly will catch little. Look for runs and try to make the most of your trapping; the more traps you have, the more vermin you will catch. And it is also a good idea to keep a note of where you have set them, or failing this tie a piece of string to a nearby convenient branch.

Traps should be sprung once a week if they have not caught. If left for too long they may well rust and fail to catch when vermin cross them.

Corvines

There are few places in Britain, even on the outskirts of suburbia, where you do not see corvines, particularly crows. During the last couple of decades the crow tribe has multiplied alarmingly and this is not just bad news for the game-preserver. The ardent non-shooting conservationist, who regularly puts out food on the bird-table in his garden, must also recognise the need for corvine control. Crows, jays and magpies do not just go hunting gamebirds' eggs and chicks; they search garden hedgerows after songbirds' nests and do immense damage to corn crops. Yet very few people are taking positive action except the shooting man. He may spend hours decoying crows with a rubber crow and owl decoy, used in conjunction with a crow-call, but his time, efforts and expense count for little if his neighbour is allowing the birds to breed unhindered on the adjacent farm.

Why have corvines bred so prolifically over the last few years? It is largely due to the decline in the numbers of full-time gamekeepers, stemming from the break-up of the private estates. Commercial farming on a large scale is not conducive to either game-preservation or conservation. Acres of corn or grassland have deprived the keeper of cover where he can trap or shoot, often extensive farmland goes unkeepered. Keepering, too, has changed; these days pressure is on the keeper to rear intensively which means that his time between May and August is devoted almost entirely to incubators, brooders and release-pens. He has little scope to maintain a network of traps or shoot corvines. Financial cut-backs have meant fewer under-keepers and assistants who might have devoted some time to vermin-control.

It is a short-sighted policy but syndicates try and make up for losses by

Crow and owl decoys for the purpose of decoying corvines. (Photo: Lance Smith)

vermin by rearing extra birds. On balance they may end up with the same number of birds after casualties but the vermin goes unchecked.

Thus it is up to every sportsman who rents his own patch to contribute to vermin-control, particularly crows. In severe weather a crow-trap can be effective. This is a simple device constructed from posts and wire mesh, a 6 feet by 6 feet cage with a tapering tunnel leading down into it. The trap is kept baited, the corvines drop down the tunnel to feed, but in order to leave they must fly back up the funnel which is impossible because of their wing-span. The captives must be despatched daily.

Rats

Rats are the curse, not just of the shoot, but of civilisation in general. The cost of the damage they do to feedstuffs annually runs into millions of pounds; it is not just what they eat but that which they spoil with their droppings. They spread disease, are a fire-risk where they gnaw through electric cables, and are a menace to poultry. Once I lost a gosling to rats, a bird which was four times the size of its killers.

I am constantly looking in my poultry houses for the first tell-tale sign of rats, a heap of fresh earth like a molehill where they have burrowed their way in. Once, some years ago, we were losing eggs to rats and I deliberately put down a nest of crock eggs – which disappeared! These were later found in the tunnels beneath the floor. A rat will roll an egg into its hole for later consumption.

Rats must be destroyed at all times. The only redeeming feature I can find in the brown rat is that it can give some good sport in a variety of ways. Years ago most of the hayricks in a farmyard contained their share of rodents and these were bolted with ferrets to be met with an army of terriers, and those rats which escaped the dogs were either killed with sticks or .410s.

Flooding is another effective means of rat control. Search out all the rat holes in an outbuilding and block them up with the exception of one; into this remaining burrow insert a hosepipe and flood the warrens beneath the floor. Provided there is no unseen escape route the whole colony of rats will be drowned.

However, if you have no wish to indulge in sport with rats, only to rid your premises or game-preserves of them, the most efficient time-saving way is by the use of bait. Over the years rats have become immune to various warfarin mixtures and there is always the need for an up-dated poison. I use *Neosorexa* which comes in the form of green crystals. This is fed to the rats in tunnels, carefully sited so that no domestic animals can get at them. On one occasion when a colony of rats moved into my poultry houses they were cleared within ten days.

With the approach of nesting time the amateur gamekeeper must ensure that there are as few rats as possible on the shoot. They will steal eggs, young chicks, foul your feedstuff. Bait early, don't wait for the rats to breed first. A sure place to poison rats is by water, so have a few baited tunnels in close proximity to your flight ponds or streams. Usually rats move into farm outbuildings with the onset of winter but I have also known them converge on poultry houses in a dry summer simply to drink from the water-hoppers. Then they discover corn and eggs and you have a problem on your hands. But whatever weapons you use in the war against rats there is nothing to beat a good cat.

Cats on the game preserves

Nowadays we have more cats than rats on our smallholding. I do not know many shooting men or gamekeepers who are fond of cats and I am inclined to think that this creature has been traditionally dubbed a rogue by generations of keepers, the depredations of the odd feral cat bringing the rest of the species into disrepute. I remember when I was a boy an old gamekeeper once told me, 'the only good cat is a dead 'un'. Likewise the keepers of old used to kill birds of prey indiscriminately, quoting the old maxim that 'if it has a hooked beak, kill it!' A short-sighted inbred policy that only present day understanding of wildlife has, hopefully, eradicated.

I have never wilfully harmed a domestic cat and I feel that to do so is unjustifiable; the majority of domestic cats are loved by somebody, especially children, and to kill one will doubtless cause family heartbreak somewhere. A cat's life is more important than that of the odd pheasant.

We have four cats which reside in close proximity to all our rearing. On one or two occasions we have rushed outside upon hearing an alarmed squawking to witness one of our cats stalking a brood of chicks, but they do not appear to be intent upon any actual harm. It is more of a game and in the end the cat grows tired of it and goes off ratting or mousing elsewhere. Our cats, hens and chicks share the same buildings and if there is any aggression it comes from the hens! Twice I have witnessed an irate Silky hen mother attack a cat without provocation, and once one of these birds put my Springer spaniel to flight. Mother hens are more than capable of looking after themselves and their brood.

Only once have I known a cat actually catch a chick and it wasn't one of our cats! The animal in question belonged to a neighbour and she returned home with a chick in her mouth which she deposited at the top of the stairs and then lost all interest in it. The chick was duly returned to its mother unharmed.

When birds grow to poult-size cats rarely take the slightest interest in them. On one occasion, after the rearing season was over, I came upon one of our cats lying quite happily up against a hen on the lawn, one sunny afternoon, with a batch of poults pecking away close by, totally unconcerned.

Cats have become very much a part of the gamekeeping scene here and I

The domestic cat does little damage on the game preserves. (Photo: Lance Smith)

would not be without them. I am firmly of the opinion that they are beneficial to game-rearing in that they control rats. I take good care not to set any fox snares near to the fields they hunt; much as I hate foxes I prefer a live cat to the possibility of a dead fox. Likewise, I would not tolerate any gamekeeper snaring my cats nor having them pursued by a pack of hounds. In either case I would ensure that the incident came to the notice of the media and I would also seek restitution.

Feral cats

Feral cats are an entirely different proposition altogether. They are wild and fierce, untameable, and will ravage a pen of young pheasants if they find a way in. They are mostly 'dumped' cats, pets which children have grown tired of and parents have taken the easy way out, put pussy in a carton and loosed her in a remote area of the countryside on the traditional Sunday afternoon spin, far enough from home so that she will not find her way back. Consequently the poor creature is faced with survival in the wild and anything edible is fair game. It learns to hunt and kill, reverts to the wild with all the cunning of the Scottish wild cat.

A few years ago we had such a beast in the vicinity of our smallholding. One winter's evening we were disturbed by a fearful noise outside, and upon going to investigate with a torch we saw this cat crouching in the long grass about twenty yards away, snarling at us. Twice after that we were awoken in the night by its fearsome screechings; it appeared to have taken up residence in a huge Forestry Commission planting, and at one stage I did actually wonder if it was a true wild cat for its markings were virtually identical to the Scottish animal. I saw it a couple more times after that and then it disappeared and was not seen again.

Feral cats should be shot; it is in the interests of your gamebirds and is also an act of mercy. But you must be absolutely sure that the creature is feral and not take a shot at a cat you see roaming your coverts. In some cases the inexperienced amateur gamekeeper may blame a cat for the crimes of foxes and roaming dogs; he should not jump to conclusions on those occasions when he comes upon a pile of feathers. The cat has, for too long, been a handy scapegoat.

Rearing

You have worked hard on your new rough shoot; with gun and traps you have taken a toll of the vermin, built a strong sizeable release pen and now you are ready to commence rearing some pheasants.

There are two methods of rearing. There is the old-fashioned open-field system where eggs are hatched under broody hens and the mother does all the

Hatching pheasant eggs in an incubator. (Photo: David Cluett; courtesy: M. G. Walker & Son)

Incubator-hatched pheasant chicks in a brooder. (Photo: David Cluett; courtesy: M. G. Walker & Son)

*Pheasant eggs vary in size. (Photo: David Cluett;
courtesy: M. G. Walker & Son)*

*The modern rearing-field. (Photo: David Cluett;
courtesy: M. G. Walker & Son)*

work. Or there is the intensive method where eggs are hatched in an incubator and the chicks are then reared in a brooder with a lamp for heat. The latter is the most widely used today because often one man can cope with several thousand birds within a confined space, whereas on the rearing-field broody hens have to be taken off the eggs and fed and watered every day, and once the chicks are hatched the pens have to be moved on to fresh grass daily.

Organised shoots and commercial game-farms opt for the intensive system in order to get maximum results. Losses must be minimal.

However, the small shoot owner will find that with only a few birds to rear the assistance of a broody hen will be beneficial. I always rear this way and will describe my own method in detail for the benefit of the beginner. However, there are various modifications but for the man with just a hundred acres, or even less, he should begin in a modest way, his target twenty or thirty birds.

I use double coops with runs attached. This means I can sit two broodies under the same roof although they are segregated from each other. There is no doubt in my mind that the Silky hen is the best sitter of all. Some may argue that one cannot put enough eggs under one, but far better to have a good hatch out of a small clutch and a good mother to look after the chicks.

Buy some eggs from a *reliable* source. By paying a little extra at a bona-fide game-farm you will have a good foundation to work on. Infertile eggs, or eggs that have been lying around unturned for a week or two, will only serve to dishearten the amateur. Where there is a choice of breed I always go for melanistic mutants. I find that these birds are less inclined to wander than the others. If you can get hold of the odd Chinese pheasant egg it is a good idea to try and hatch one or two of these light-coloured birds along with the rest. When fully grown they are easily spotted in field or covert and give you a good idea of the movements of the rest of your pheasants.

With the eggs under the broodies you should have it easy for a while, just a case of feeding and watering the hens. Once the chicks have hatched you will need to feed them on starter crumbs. Ensure that you purchase *pheasant* crumbs; ordinary chick crumbs will not have the necessary protein and turkey crumbs are uncertain. Recently a notice was displayed in the office of my local mill to the effect that gamekeepers feeding pheasants on turkey starter crumbs might suffer heavy mortality rates. Apparently this was due to the extra protein needed by pheasants not being included in the turkey crumbs.

I mix corn and crumbs together in equal proportions and feed to hen and chicks. If you feed them in separate containers the hen will usually eat the crumbs first; mix them up and she scratches them all over the floor and the chicks will have plenty of scope to help themselves. Fresh water is essential; I use an old remedy of including a drop of TCP in the drinking water as a precaution against gapes. Prevention is better than cure.

An old-fashioned rearing field. (Photo: Lance Smith)

The Silky hen is the best mother of all. (Photo: Lance Smith)

Feather-pecking

Feather-pecking is the curse of most penned birds, whether pheasants, hens or turkeys. I am not a believer in artificial attachments such as 'specs' to prevent this. Neither do I like de-beaking. You are attempting to introduce a wild bird into the wild so the more natural the process is, the better.

I suspend a lettuce or two from the roof of the pen and this occupies them for a while but a batch of pheasants will consume a lettuce right down to the stalk in a matter of minutes. Feather-pecking is caused by boredom, and once there is bare and bleeding flesh showing on a bird the rest will not let it alone. I have used mirrors in the pen to some degree of success; the poults are intrigued by their own reflection, believing it to be other birds but are curious because their efforts to peck meet with a hard invisible barrier.

At six weeks the poults should go to the release-pen in the wood. If you have done your groundwork thoroughly you need have no fears about their safety although they will need constant supervision. Pheasants will do all manner of silly and unbelievable things.

I remember checking my release-pen one evening and noting with some surprise a cock pheasant's tail feather sticking up out of the ground like a growing plant. My first thought was that a cock bird had lost its tail and that somehow the quill had become embedded in the ground. On closer investigation I discovered that the tail was, in fact, still attached to the bird which was securely stuck down a rabbit hole! With some difficulty I freed the captive; it had obviously sought to escape from constant bullying by another male bird and in desperation had tried to go underground.

The poults will need to settle after their move to their larger quarters and the less you go inside the pen for the first few days, the better. Ensure that they have ample water and food and in due course begin some hand-feeding because you want the pheasants to associate you and the release-pen with food.

You want the birds to learn to go up to roost each evening, for when eventually they desert the pen for the wild this will be their only nocturnal protection against foxes. Owls can be a nuisance, not so much because they will kill the odd bird but because they can disturb roosting pheasants, and a poult which tumbles from its perch in the night will 'juk' on the ground where it is quite likely to be found by Reynard.

I am not in favour of erecting a flashing light in the region of a pen full of pheasants. Your aforementioned defences should be ample but a light is likely to attract the attention of poachers and thieves who will clear your birds in one raid.

I generally leave it a fortnight before I open up the entrance–exit tunnels and offer the poults a chance to explore beyond their wire-mesh boundary. Leave them to their own devices but keep an eye on them. They will forage

Pheasants may not always be acceptable on SSSI-designated land.
(Photo: Lance Smith)

and return later in the day because the pen is their home.

That main central wide ride through the wood can now be littered with straw and you can start scattering grain in this, for eventually the birds will forsake the pen and they must learn that there will always be food here. Or else they will stray, make no mistake about that. Now you will need to concentrate all your tunnel-trapping on this area for an abundance of grain will attract grey squirrels and rats.

Ex-laying birds

This is often the layman's short-cut to a busy rearing programme or perhaps a means of making up losses. Every July game-farmers offer the bulk of their adult laying birds for sale, often at prices that are competitive with six-week-old poults. You may think that this is the easy way out, you do not have to go to all the trouble of eggs, chicks, rearing disasters. In some ways this is true, and you get what you pay for. Your losses will be small but your birds will be prone to straying.

They are not poults growing up in a new environment; they are fully-grown birds who know all about the wild and they want their freedom.

Whatever else you may save on, you will need a release-pen because these birds will have to be kept penned for several weeks until they accept their new surroundings. If you have not got a roof on your pen you must brail your birds or else they will fly out over the top and that is the last you will see of them.

In the event of your opting for an ex-layers programme, buy at the ratio of one cock to at least a dozen hens. Too many cocks in a confined space will fight and often kill one another.

However, there *is* a bonus to adult birds. Some of the hens will still be laying and I have known very late broods on shoots which have been the result of hens going down to sit. But, on balance, you will do better with poults. Most important, you will learn the gamekeeper's job from first-hand experience. One never stops learning.

Ringing

It is well worthwhile going to the trouble of putting rings on your birds. You will know then whether the birds you shoot are your own or whether they are wild birds. Or perhaps a neighbour's which have strayed over the boundary. And your neighbour will know too!

Numbered rings are even better because by keeping concise records it is possible to tell when pheasants have survived a season and are shot the next. If you shoot a number of last year's birds then you are progressing, increasing the potential of the shoot. You have obviously done your vermin-control well, your shoot is conducive to game and there is little, if any, poaching going on.

Partridges

You can rear partridges in much the same way as pheasants except that the release point has to be in arable cover such as a field of roots. You will need to feed heavily to keep the coveys from hopping over the hedge into an identical neighbouring field of swedes.

Holding partridge is the main difficulty, particularly on a small acreage, and my advice to the beginner is to begin with pheasants and survey the partridge scene.

As I have already stated, partridge love old pastureland which is why a covey always frequent my land in preference to a larger acreage of sprayed farmland. As one farmer remarked to me a short time ago, 'them old partridge don't seem to be getting any more, do they? I suppose it's these sprays.'

Never was a truer word spoken.

Shooting

Finally autumn arrives and now is the time to reap the harvest of all your spring and summer work. You have earned it but that is no excuse for being greedy. Remember, you are a conservationist as well as a sportsman and your main objective is to build up and *maintain* a stock of game.

Farmer Jones has no objection to your bringing a companion along. And don't forget, even though the farmer may have given up shooting several years ago, extend an invitation to him to join you.

You must plan your shooting days carefully, taking into consideration your boundaries. Always try and drive your birds in a 'homeward' direction, which isn't easy on a small shoot. Avoid shooting close to that release-pen and your main feeding area, regard it as a kind of sanctuary because if the pheasants become accustomed to not being shot at there they will invariably head back to it.

Where do you begin the day? If you have some water on the land which holds duck then this is the obvious place to start because the duck will be up and away at the first shot.

Colonel Peter Hawker did not shoot in roots until after ten o'clock in the morning. Sound advice, for just stop and think how the pheasant organises *his* day. He will drop down from roost at first light and feed on the grain you have scattered on the ride. His crop full, he has an urge to wander elsewhere

Pheasants which are not hand fed will stray. (Photo: Lance Smith)

57

and the field of swedes offers inviting cover. Maybe on wet days he will skulk in the hedgerows, if there are any which have not been massacred by a flail-cutter! But the roots are always worth a try as I have already related. Walk upwind and pray that the wind is not blowing from your neighbour's hedgerow.

You feel very satisfied at putting a brace in the bag, your own reared birds; your chosen plan of action has proved to be the right one, and now perhaps you can try that small spinney, quarter of a mile from your 'home covert'. Your aim again is to drive any birds either back to the big wood or else into the roots which you have already worked. If they plane down into the latter, leave them there. It is not good policy to harass birds.

Your programme should be a reasonably casual one. A hurrying shooter walks past squatting birds and often misses those he flushes. Besides, it is a day you want to savour. Allow your dog to work thoroughly; usually he has a better idea of where birds are than you have.

During the winter months, when the days are short, it is detrimental to any shoot to pursue pheasants up until dusk. By three o'clock in the afternoon they are thinking about going home for a last feed on the big ride and then flying up to roost. They should be allowed to do so. One drive too many could result in them going to roost in somebody else's wood and they might decide next morning that they like it better there after all!

Perhaps you will finish the day with a duck-flight back at the pond. Or maybe flighting pigeon, but take care that it is well away from your main pheasant roosting area.

So a very satisfying day comes to an end. Don't forget to bid the farmer goodnight on your departure, and if you have a bird to spare offer it to him.

You are one of the lucky ones. By diligent and intelligent searching you have found your shoot and are already managing it successfully. But you cannot rest on your laurels. Shoot management is a twelve months of the year job. For the moment you can relax and enjoy your sport but with the advent of February it will be time to start all over again.

CHAPTER FIVE

Syndicate Shooting

Let us go back to that initial meeting with our Farmer Jones. Everything is fine, he is willing to rent the shooting of his farm to you but there is one big difference. Instead of his acreage being a mere 100 to 200, it is much larger, say 800. You were not aware that he had recently bought the adjacent farm for his son who is no longer interested in shooting either. So even a fair rental is more than you can afford. The only solution is to form a syndicate and share the upkeep and the gamekeeping duties.

There are two ways in which a syndicate might be run.

1. You decide that the shoot has potential but cannot afford to run it. So you pay the rent yourself and the lease is in your name. You then 'sell' an equal number of guns who pay their share to you, plus the running costs. In effect they are your paying guests. In this way you assume total responsibility for the running of the shoot. Fine if all goes well, but after a poor season you may well have your guests complaining and blaming you for the failure.

2. You gather together a number of suitable guns and agree to share the total running costs and rental. The shoot is then run by a *team* of organisers, and success or failure will be shared.

For preference I would choose the latter method but there is an awful lot to be considered before you commit yourself.

Choosing guns

No shoot will be a success without suitable guns and much thought must be given to this before your prospective 'founder members' join you in a preliminary meeting. The guns will be the focal point of the whole season and one unsuitable one can spoil it for everybody else.

You have agreed a rental with the farmer and decided that a total of six guns will be adequate. Work out your running costs; pheasant eggs, an incubator and brooder, feedstuffs, beginning with starter crumbs right up to corn for feeding the woods, and don't forget that you do not stop feeding the moment the season is over. Your remaining stock of birds, if not caught up for laying, must be encouraged to remain and hopefully breed in the wild. Eventually you arrive at a rough figure and now all you need is five other sportsmen to pay their share.

One frequently sees advertisements in the sporting press, 'full gun available in mixed shoot, ten days guaranteed', or 'half-gun required for pheasant shoot'. The latter will only pay a half-share and as such will only shoot on half the number of allotted days.

If you advertise then you will have to interview each applicant very carefully but in fact you will not really find out about those you accept into your shoot until you begin shooting with them.

Safety is of paramount importance. Where a number of guns shoot together you cannot afford to take any risks. You must beware of the *nouveau riche*, the man who has become successful in his particular line of business and decides he needs a sport where he is likely to meet useful business contacts. Or merely to shoot as a status symbol. You need to know his background; how long he has been shooting, where he last shot, etc. This may seem hard on the beginner and there is no reason why you should not accept a novice, *providing his attitude is right*. There is no hard and fast rule for recognising the man who wants to shoot for the sake of the sport. Ask a few questions, let him talk as much as he wants to, try to sum him up.

Carrying the gun safely when not expecting a shot. (Photo: Lance Smith)

Possibly you have a few friends in mind. But will they blend into a team? You feel sorry for Bill because he, like yourself, has been searching for somewhere to shoot for a long time. Is he a loner, would he fit in with a party? And you must not disregard the social side of the shoot because if the syndicate is to work you cannot just meet a few times during the winter months and then go your separate ways. You have to organise and co-operate with each other and the last thing you want is a private feud between two members.

Interview each prospective gun as you would do applicants for a job you have on offer. Don't make a hasty decision. If you know of five suitable sportsmen who fit the bill then you are very lucky.

A preliminary meeting is essential once you have chosen your guns. This is probably the most important meeting you will ever hold in the history of your syndicate and every major point must be raised. It is as well to over-estimate the costs rather than to have to ask for more money later on. Once everybody has paid up the money should be put into a separate banking account where close watch can be kept on the finances.

The first step after that is to appoint a shoot captain for the year. This can be done by voting; the shoot must be run democratically if you are to maintain harmony but there must be somebody in charge. The post can be taken in turn amongst you, beginning with a new captain each February.

At this initial meeting, apart from finances, you must establish how many birds you are going to rear and how many days you are going to shoot. The two are related; if you do not rear many pheasants, you cannot shoot every week. If you overshoot, you will have run out of birds by Christmas, just when the sport ought to be reaching its peak. Guns will then be disheartened by poor days and the good ones will be forgotten. Better a few memorable days than a number best forgotten.

The gamekeeper

Who is going to control the vermin and rear the pheasants? Are you going to take on a part-time keeper in return for shooting with the syndicate or are you going to attend to all the keepering duties yourselves? Unless you know of a reliable part-time keeper the latter is the safest bet. But if the shoot is some distance from your homes then you will need a man on the spot.

This again will be a question of choosing the right man which is not easy in a distant locality. For the majority of the time he will have a free hand and if birds disappear then who is to argue that they have not strayed or been poached? Where possible the keepering should be a shared d.i.y. job. But you must make it clear at the outset that every member must pull his weight. The duty rota must be drawn up in writing and strictly observed. If the man responsible for feeding the pheasants in the woods neglects his job then those birds will have strayed in a matter of a week.

Vermin-control can be a combined effort. On weekends during February and March you can meet just as you have throughout the season; only now your quarry will be corvines and grey squirrels. The alternative to sharing the gamekeeper's job is appointing a keeper amongst yourselves, perhaps on an annual basis along with the captain. That is fine so long as the man concerned has some experience. But it does not mean that the rest of you can forget all about the shoot until September arrives.

Your keeper, whoever he is, will need help even on the most professionally-run shoot. Whenever possible you should turn up to give him a hand. All of you must learn his duties because accident or illness could befall him in the midst of the rearing-season.

Shooting days

Having established how many days you are going to shoot, much planning is necessary for each of those days. Conditions will alter as autumn blends into winter; the roots will have been harvested or the sheep turned in to strip-graze them and cover will be lost. The starting point in October may well be the finishing point in January.

Every member should have a map of the shoot and this will be invaluable in planning your days. As with the small rough-shoot your aim is to drive your birds in a homeward direction wherever possible.

Beaters

You must determine at the outset whether to hire beaters or to alternate between walking and standing guns amongst yourselves. Largely this will be determined by the number of birds you have released and the shoot finances. Beaters will expect about £5 per day, their lunch included and perhaps some item of game to take home. Unless yours is an average 60–100 birds-per-day shoot I would think that beaters are a luxury you cannot afford. Cheap beating can often be obtained via members' families, relations who enjoy a day spent thus, or by offering pigeon shooting to aspiring shooters once the season is over. There are several perks one can offer in return for casual beating.

However on the small syndicate shoot walking-up can often be combined with driving *but safety must be foremost*. Where there are standing guns then *everybody* must be aware of their exact position and the former must be instructed that on no account are they to move position. No low shots must be taken by either standing or walking guns except for birds breaking back.

Picking-up

There are invariably willing volunteers, keen gundog enthusiasts, who welcomed the opportunity to pick-up. Their presence will be an asset to the shoot but their dogs must know what they are about. Unruly dogs can spoil the day for everybody and only trained dogs should be invited to participate. You need to vet your pickers-up in much the same way as you interviewed the guns who now shoot with you.

The first task at the end of every drive is to retrieve all game shot. This is a duty which must not be delayed for a wounded pheasant will be intent on putting as much distance between himself and the shooting party as possible. The guns must be patient and allow the dogs time to work.

Likewise, after a Saturday shoot, it is well worthwhile returning to the scene of the various drives with your dog on a Sunday morning. There will be strong runners which have not been gathered, and apart from the waste of edible game you owe it to the birds to gather them rather than leave them to a lingering death.

I make no apologies for stressing once again that shooting should cease by mid-afternoon during the winter months to allow the pheasants time to go back to roost in peace. I have noticed on several syndicate shoots to which I have been invited that a duck-flight is an optional extra. Often nobody bothers; perhaps they have had their fill but more likely it is the social side of the shooting day which takes precedence.

The social side

It is necessary to have some kind of a break during the shooting which has commenced at 9.30 am but if sport is to cease by 3 o'clock then a full meal in the middle of the day will waste valuable time; also it is not conducive to good shooting. Alcohol should not feature in the sporting scene until after the close. A shotgun is a lethal weapon and marred judgement is highly dangerous.

Most syndicates cater for a meal of some kind at the end of the day. On the larger shoots where there is a full-time resident keeper it is often his wife's perk to cook a dinner for the syndicate. The cost per head is worked out and each member pays for his meal but don't forget an adequate tip for the good lady who has worked for hours to lay on the spread. A cash kitty is a good idea for drinks, each one chipping-in a fiver when the 'bar' is running low.

On smaller shoots an arrangement can usually be made with a local pub to provide a meal after the shoot. Often landlords welcome this because it is extra income and at a convenient time of the day between afternoon closing and evening opening. The syndicate will be able to eat in private in a relaxed atmosphere.

I believe that such gatherings are important to the running of the shoot.

The day's sport can be discussed in detail and mistakes ironed out. It gives everybody an opportunity to put forward their ideas.

Perhaps an invitation to wives and girlfriends to join you for dinner will add to the convivial atmosphere. All too often the ladies become 'shooting widows' during the winter months and the chance to become part of the shooting scene will ensure their co-operation. For them Saturdays will not then become that boring day of the week when they are left to their own devices, perhaps without even a vehicle in which to go shopping or visiting friends.

Christmastime must be something a little special. The festive shoot should have an additional atmosphere about it. A roast turkey instead of the usual pheasant or whatever, even an evening out at a local hotel. Some of the larger shoots organise a dinner-dance but if your syndicate does not run to that then you can always arrange to meet up somewhere just to make it that little bit different. Monotonous routine can detract from the pleasures of shooting.

Disposal of game

The bag at the end of the day is what it is all about. Whatever the quality of the sport, Man is a hunter and his efforts have provided a valuable supply of food. Arrangements for the disposal of game must be made at the outset of the season and adhered to.

Every member should be entitled to a brace of birds and an additional choice of 'various' such as duck, rabbit, hare, etc. On the small d.i.y syndicate shoot this will usually account for the head shot but on larger shoots there will surely be a surplus. As the finances need to be strictly controlled in order to keep costs down, the sale of game can provide a useful source of income and the proceeds should be paid into the bank account so that they are not swallowed up in other hidden expenses.

It is important to keep a close watch on fluctuating game prices, though. Deal only with a reputable game-dealer or hotel and don't leave this until November when you begin shooting pheasants in earnest. You want the best possible prices for your birds. However, any shoot member who wishes to buy an additional brace of birds at the dealer's prices should be allowed to do so.

I have come across syndicates where there are no complimentary birds for members at the end of the day; if you want a brace then you have to buy them. No way would I join any syndicate on those terms. It is akin to digging somebody else's garden and then buying a cabbage off him to take home. In that situation I would purchase a brace from the local poulterer and find something else to do on Saturday afternoons. It is yet another way of exploiting the sportsman.

Whether your game is going to the dealer or being shared out amongst the guns, *presentation* is important. As soon as possible after each drive birds should be hung up; a game-rack in the back of a vehicle is ideal for this. Scruffy pheasants piled in a heap is nothing short of an insult to a noble bird. If you have time, brush the feathers, give your quarry a little dignity in death in return for the sport it has given you in life. Little finishing touches such as this enhance the glamour of a day's shooting.

Game should be hung in as cool a place as possible. Where feasible delegate a beater to return them to base at intervals during the day, particularly in the earlier, warmer months of the season. And ensure that they are kept under lock and key; I have heard of more than one instance where the party have retired for lunch only to find the game-larder bare.

Everybody has their personal preferences for how they like to eat their game. Traditionally partridges and pheasants and other gamebirds should be hung for up to two or three weeks before eating. I find this quite revolting but everybody to their own taste. Hanging game stems from pre-refrigeration days when, after a shoot where there was a surplus of game, it was impossible to preserve it in any other way than by hanging in a cool cellar until it was eaten. So our ancestors became accustomed to meat that was high and strong and handed this recipe down over the generations. In effect they were consuming decomposing flesh. I like my game as fresh as possible; everything is plucked and dressed on the day following at the very latest, and birds shot prior to Thursday and destined for the Sunday lunch table are frozen until Saturday. There are no hard and fast rules, it is all a question of how *you* like to eat your game. It is best to experiment for yourself, not blindly follow the advice of others.

Rabbits should be gutted as soon as possible after being killed but hares should be left intact until they are skinned. The game cookbooks advocate eating snipe and woodcock undrawn with the heads left on so that the beaks can be used as a skewer; I prefer mine dressed in the same way as a pheasant or partridge.

Joining an established syndicate

Let us now look at the other side of the coin: *you* are the one looking to join an established syndicate. You have not been successful in finding your own small shoot, neither have you come across a larger acreage from which you could form your syndicate. You decide to look round for a reasonably-priced gun in the *right* syndicate for you.

Unless you hear of an available gun by word of mouth you will have to watch the advertisement columns of the various shooting magazines carefully. Your priority will be a vacancy within reasonable motoring distance of your home and one that your pocket can stand. In all probability you will have to settle for a half-gun until you have weighed up the syndicate in question and accept that the first season will be one during which you will also be on trial.

Having made contact, the next step will be an interview. My advice here is to be perfectly honest and avoid pretensions. If you feign experience you will be found out before very long. However, the interview should not be a one-sided affair because there is a lot *you* need to know also. Basically, the information you require is:

1. The overall cost with an approximation of 'hidden expenses', keepers' tips if applicable, your share of the cost of eggs, chicks, equipment, etc.

2. How many days shooting you can expect.

3. What duties are expected of you if there is no full-time gamekeeper.

You should make the acquaintance of the syndicate members as soon as conveniently possible.

Most of the larger shoots have 'formal' and 'informal' days. On the former there will be beaters, properly organised drives and usually a full meal afterwards. But the latter are usually walked-up affairs, or the guns taking it in turn to beat. Make sure that you get everything you are entitled to; you have paid your subscription, don't be talked into accepting an informal day for one of your formal ones just because one of the existing members decides he has an influential business acquaintance whom he would like to invite.

Etiquette

Shooting etiquette is of great importance, especially on those formal days. Really it is common sense. You carry your gun 'broken' (open at the breech) and unloaded between all drives. You only shoot at birds which are in range of your own stand and you don't shoot at low-flying or immature pheasants. In most instances the keeper will signal the start of a drive with a whistle and close it likewise. Never be tempted to take a bird before or after.

You will be expected to dress appropriately. This means that if you have been accustomed to going rough-shooting in any old garments you must now be clad smartly. There is a variety of sporting headgear on the market and style is flexible but, like the rest of your clothing, it must blend in with your surroundings. Your jacket must fit you properly and not impede your shooting. You need two ideally, a light showerproof one for the early weeks of the season and a waterproof one for the latter part and pouring wet days. If you don't like wearing breeches or plus-fours you can settle for moleskins or cords. As I have already mentioned, cheap green wellington boots look quite acceptable in the shooting field but may not suit everybody. A good gunshop will stock most of your requirements but shop around before buying.

Ensure that you turn up promptly for every shoot. There is nothing more annoying than late guns who delay the first drive. Late arrivals can spoil it for everybody; the guns will have drawn for pegs and the stand left over will

Guns must be carried 'broken' in between drives. (Photo: Lance Smith)

be the absentee's. In the event of an unavoidable delay, you will have to sit-out the first drive for you cannot go walking along the line looking for your place amidst the shooting.

Ascertain beforehand whether or not you can bring your dog. If you are allowed to do so then he will be expected to remain with you throughout the day and only go picking-up when requested.

And don't forget to tip the keeper at the end of the day. Apart from expressing you appreciation of his efforts, remember that his wage is not a lucrative one and tips are one of the gamekeeper's perks. Discreetly find out from the other guns how much they give him, and do likewise.

Guest days

You may or may not be entitled to a guest day. If you are only a half-gun it is unlikely but in the event of you being awarded one during the course of the season it is something that needs thinking about carefully.

That pal of yours who often used to accompany you on the rough-shoot or invited you to his, would he be acceptable on a formal day's shooting? By acceptable, I mean from an etiquette and general sportsmanship angle.

It is a fact that a good shot will earn himself many more invitations than a mediocre or poor one, as will the owner of a dog with a reputation for being steady and finding wounded game. Some members of syndicates are notoriously poor shots, much to the gamekeeper's chagrin, and a guest who is an above-average marksman will be more than welcome. Once pheasant shooting gets into full swing around November the syndicate like to make some good bags. It boosts the finances of the shoot and is a reward for money invested during the rearing-season. I make no criticism of large bags where game is reared; I deplore a slaughter of wild birds or a neighbour's straying game by selfish shooters who give nothing in return for what they take. One must first sow in order to reap a harvest.

If perchance you are indisposed with one of your shooting days imminent, then you should consult the captain of the shoot regarding a replacement. Possibly he will leave it up to you to fill the gap by inviting that friend who shot so well last month. Whatever you decide between you, every effort should be taken to find a replacement for a gun short can seriously hamper plans. There will be a blank peg at every drive and it could just be that the pheasants will stream over that vacant post unshot at.

Pick up your fired cases

You should not need reminding to pick up your fired cases at the end of every drive. Just as you would not dream of throwing down an empty cigarette packet in the street, so you must not litter the countryside with empty cartridges.

Plastic-cased cartridges do not rot down. Apart from the unsightliness, they are dangerous to livestock. Cattle and sheep are remarkably silly creatures and cartridge cases are not easily digested!

Shooting by invitation

There are some sportsmen who rely entirely upon invitations for their shooting. They can be divided into three categories:

1. The businessman who has not the time available either to join a syndicate or rent some shooting of his own.

2. The ardent prospective shooting man who, in spite of all his efforts, has not yet succeeded in finding a shoot for himself and cannot afford to join a syndicate.

3. The selfish shooter who is unwilling to pay for his sport but is quite happy to enjoy someone else's.

The latter we can discard immediately; he does not deserve any shooting and his invitations will peter out altogether once his acquaintances realise what he is up to. The businessman is excusable; doubtless he will repay his hosts in other ways and more than likely they have something to gain by asking him along.

The one searching for some shooting, handicapped financially but not giving up, deserves our sympathy. He will fully appreciate a day on the shoot but if he is a genuine sportsman he will be secretly embarrassed because he has no way of repaying his understanding host. Or has he?

Put yourself in this luckless man's position. Farmer Jones refused to let you his small farm and your efforts to form a syndicate for a larger acreage fell through. Bitterly disappointed, you have equipped yourself accordingly and your dog is fretting because no shooting is coming along. Then, out of the blue, comes a phone call from your friend, whose finances are considerably better than yours, and who has a gun in a well-known syndicate a few miles from your home.

Next Saturday is his allocated guest day and would you like a day's shooting? There are five drives; be at the Lodge at 9.15 for a prompt start at 9.30. A break for a quick cup of coffee at 12 noon and finish shooting at 2.30. And there will be a meal laid on by the keeper's wife in the tack-house at 3 o'clock.

Your pulses race, you can barely get a wink of sleep on the eve of the big day. From being unable even to find some vermin shooting you have been plunged into the cream of the sport. The Estate has a reputation for 100-bird-plus days and tomorrow is the first time through the Home Covert. Will you be on form? It is weeks since you last fired your gun at the local clay-pigeon club and you didn't do awfully well on that occasion.

If you are schooled in shooting etiquette then you have little to worry about. Most shoots really look after their guests and your friend will be there to advise you. Try and relax, you won't perform well if you are tense. You are in the draw for pegs along with everybody else, including your host, and you find yourself in the 'pound seat' for the main drive of the day. Nineteen birds down out of thirty shots; you are euphoric. The meal is superb and your only regret is that you are unable to reciprocate because you don't have any shooting in return. But there are other ways . . .

Shoots are always grateful for the additional volunteer beater and in a small way you can repay your friend by expressing a desire to beat. You will also benefit from witnessing a big shoot from the beater's point of view.

Beating

The beaters are an integral part of the shoot. Without them driven game would be impossible, the quality of the sport and the size of the bag would be much reduced.

Yet beating is not merely a question of walking blindly through woodlands or roots; pheasants, particularly hand-reared ones, are reluctant to fly if they can possibly avoid it. They will run, squat, try to break back behind the beaters as if they know that ahead a line of guns is waiting for them.

A lazy beater will avoid a patch of briars or look for a suitable 'path' through a field of kale and will pass within feet of a skulking pheasant. The keeper, or the one in charge of the line of beaters, soon gets to know anybody unreliable. It is an arduous task beating on a wet day but if it is not carried out properly then it is a waste of time.

The beater should always be suitably clad, waterproof and thornproof clothing except during the early part of the season, and needs to carry a stick to tap trees with and to thrash thick patches of brambles. It must be an organised exercise, and the team must keep in line and not straggle. Keep an eye on the one on either side of you, make a noise, hoot or whistle or whatever takes your fancy. Few birds will flush for a silent beater.

Just because you are a willing volunteer and your friend happens to be one of the guns, don't expect any privileges. You are just one of the beaters on the day and you must do as they do, join them for their sandwich and beer lunch afterwards. But there may be other advantages which you will share in at a later date. Towards the end of the season, when the cream of the sport is over, some syndicates arrange for the beaters to have a shoot of their own in an attempt to reduce a surplus of cock birds; too many cocks left on a shoot can disrupt the nesting programme in the spring. Or, failing a game shoot, you may well be invited to join in the after-season woodpigeon battues during February and March.

It is certainly worthwhile getting in on the beating scene. And if no shooting is forthcoming as a result at least you will have been seen to reciprocate in a small way for that excellent day's sport earlier on. Whatever, beating will keep you in touch with the sport and you will learn an immense amount about the running of a shoot from it.

Farmers' shoots

During my boyhood initiation into shooting in the days when I used to accompany my father round his small rough-shoot on Saturday afternooons, he sometimes used to take me along to shoots organised by local farmers. As a bank manager he had numerous invitations during October and November and I used to trail along behind him lugging a heavy game-bag and enjoying every second of it.

Nowadays farmers' shoots are not as common as they were in the years just after the war. Principally this is due to economic agriculture which has changed the pattern of our countryside, smaller farms being sold and amalgamated into larger ones, and shooting being rented to syndicates. Farmers are busy people, most of the time they do not have time for shooting. But in those days the majority of the farmers got together for an annual sporting and social occasion once the harvest was over.

Sometimes there were as many as fifteen guns present, a formidable army tramping the fields with a variety of awesome weapons. I well remember one old farmer well into his seventies who used a rusty hammer gun, the fore-end fastened on with a piece of wire. Once, during walking-up partridge in clover, that fore-end fell off and the shoot was delayed for several minutes whilst we all searched for it. He boasted that he wore a gun out in five years and when he needed a new one he went down to the local sale-room and bought another for a couple of pounds. He was a superb shot; once he turned up with some ex-home-guard cartridges loaded with SSG shot and killed a partridge with one. The bird was decapitated by the buckshot!

Those were the shoots on which safety was virtually ignored. I still have nightmares of the day when we moved off after lunch to shoot another farm, and lying on the floor of the car in which I rode was a fully loaded and cocked hammer gun! Mercifully I never witnessed an accident.

But those shoots were conducted without any thought of conservation. Young pheasants rose in coveys and there was a burst of gunfire all down the line. Every field and hedgerow was worked and the bird that escaped was a lucky one. Generally each farmer had just one shoot, his aim being to harvest a crop of game. Yet there were always more birds about in those days, all of them wild birds because the mania for chemical spraying had not yet begun.

And, of course, there were the harvest shoots, another get-together of anybody who owned or could borrow a gun, regardless of whether or not they could shoot. If you couldn't then you soon learned because rabbits were bolting continually as the binder reduced the corn cover; everybody moved in close for that final swathe and that was generally when the remaining rabbits bolted in all directions. I once recall a farm-labourer getting 'peppered' in the leg during such a finale; there was no undue panic, one of his colleagues prised out some of the pellets with a penknife and he went to the doctor the following day!

Myxomatosis sounded the death-knell of corn shooting. With few or no rabbits bolting from the corn nobody bothered to turn up with a gun on harvest days. Then came new machinery, the combine-harvester that could gobble up a field of barley in half the time of its predecessor. The rural scene was changing, not wholly for the worse because many of those farmers began to look upon game as a worthwhile crop. It was advantageous to rear a few birds or to let the shoot for a lucrative rental. Conservation crept in slowly but at the same time chemical insecticides had already begun to decimate the partridge population. Myxomatosis cleared the rabbits, birds of prey were in danger of extinction for some years as a result. Those farmers whose dream of Utopia was a rabbitless countryside were soon disillusioned. The decline of the humble bunny made little difference to the size of the crop harvested. The partridge was conspicuous by its absence, wild pheasants fared badly. Gone were the days of carefree shooting, to be replaced by a much more artificial countryside where shooting was a commodity in demand. Rents escalated, the old rough-shoot was hard to find, familiar spinneys and thick hedgerows had been bulldozed out to make way for acres of grain to create a surplus that nobody wanted.

Yet one detects the winds of change blowing again. Some enlightened farmers are already beginning to replant woods and hedges and there is the prospect of a new era.

We can only hope.

CHAPTER SIX

Shooting by Permission Only

In my early shooting days there was a market-garden farm about half a mile from where I lived, in the centre of which was a ten-acre wood. There were always pheasants in this wood and during the winter months pigeons roosted in the tall trees in their hundreds. I knew the farmer well and he told me to go for a shot any time I wanted.

The first time I went was one snowy afternoon during the Christmas holidays; the woodies poured into that wood all afternoon and by four o'clock I was out of cartridges and was more than delighted with the few birds I had shot. It did not escape my notice, however, that the floor of this wood was littered with spent cartridge cases.

I went again the following Saturday afternoon and it was a different story then. There were at least a dozen other guns amongst the trees and every pigeon that showed up was blasted at from all directions. Some time afterwards I asked the farmer if he would be interested in letting me the shooting rights. 'Not really,' he smiled and shook his head, 'because in hard weather I like plenty of guns on the place to keep the pigeons off the cabbages. If I didn't let folks shoot all the year round I could hardly expect them to go and belt the pigeons when the snow comes. But feel free to go and shoot whenever you like.'

It was fair comment. And there are a number of farmers, particularly those who grow brassicas, who feel that way. In theory, then, the aspiring shooter should have no difficulty in obtaining a shot at pigeons and rabbits. But I'm afraid it doesn't quite work out that way today.

The reason principally is that so much shooting is let for high rentals that losses which farmers may suffer from pigeons is balanced by the income from leasing the shooting rights. Or where there is a gamekeeper he will supervise any extra vermin-control. In most cases the syndicate themselves will welcome some pigeon-shooting. All of which excludes the enthusiastic beginner.

During the 1960s, county-wide pigeon shoots were organised on Saturday afternoons during February and March, the plan being to man every available patch of woodland and keep the birds on the move. I remember

73

once our Rotary Club organising a shoot of this type. A few of the lucky sportsmen had some shooting; most saw only a few birds. The reason was clear; although gamekeepers were willing to participate they limited the number of guns around the game-preserves. Gunfire on a large scale is not good for pheasant woods even after the season is over but, more important, blanket permission to shoot is an open invitation to poachers to knock the odd pheasant off. Pigeon battues are good fun but they rarely produce large bags; at best they serve to keep the woodies off market-gardenland for one afternoon of the week. For the other six days they can feed undisturbed.

We have already looked at how pigeon-shooting is being commercialised, and the novice would do well to keep his money in his pocket unless he makes some kind of reconnaissance and ascertains that pigeons are actually feeding on the land. Even so, there is no guarantee that they will be in the same place on the following day. Personally, I would never pay for pigeon or vermin shooting anyway; you are doing the farmer a service by protecting his crops.

From time to time one sees advertisements by sportsmen offering their services in respect of pigeon control. Doubtless a good number of these are genuine offers but I would doubt if they receive much response to their advert. If one intends to set up as a professional pigeon-shooter then it is necessary to establish a reputation first in order to be able to pursue the grey flocks from farm to farm. Catch 22: how do you build up that reputation if you cannot get permission to shoot in the first place?

Really it has to be done by personal contact and word of mouth. Possibly by joining a local Gun Club you will find that members have permission to shoot vermin on specific farms and you may benefit from that. Or possibly you know somebody who decoys pigeons regularly and you could seek an invitation to accompany him, not necessarily to shoot on the first few outings but to help carry his equipment and learn how to build hides and set out decoys.

There is no short cut to permission to shoot. It is worth a try, adopting the same tactics as have been described in an earlier chapter when looking for a shoot to rent. Drive from farm to farm and ask – the farmer can only say 'no'! However, it needs to be done fairly systematically, because obtaining permission to shoot on land that is barren of pigeon is of no use.

Your first outing should be a reconnaissance with binoculars. The object is to find the pigeons! Rabbits are not so obvious and if it is rabbiting you are after then you have to rely on the word of the farmer that there are rabbits on his land, as well as obtaining permission to shoot or ferret them. First, though, let us deal with woodpigeon-shooting in more detail.

PIGEON-SHOOTING

Preparations

To what extent do you wish to shoot pigeons? On a casual, relaxed basis, either walking round a farm in search of the odd shot or waiting for them flighting in to a wood in the late afternoon? Or attempting to make a sizeable bag by decoying?

Casual pigeon-shooting rarely yields a big bag. Pigeon are not like pheasants where you can systematically walk over 100 acres or so, take your time and end up with a few in the bag. You stalk through woodland, drop a bird which clatters out of the foliage, and every other pigeon in the wood will be on the wing looking for safer quarters. Roost-shooting is uncertain. Again you need to study flight-lines beforehand and then there is no guarantee that the wind will not have changed slightly and they come in from elsewhere. In the right place at the right time you may do well, but not as well as you would do with decoys in the right place. Pigeon provide excellent sport, akin to wildfowling; they offer testing shots, have the keenest of eyesight and will spot you at once if you are not suitably camouflaged, and your 'Big Day' might arrive without warning. That is half the fun of shooting woodies: they are so unpredictable.

Equipment

Clothing is of vital importance and you are not allowed the choice which the game-shooter enjoys. *A hat with a brim is a must* because your face will show up against most backgrounds. Ex-army camouflage clothing is fine with hat, jacket and trousers to match. Except in snow when you will need a lighter garment; I have used an old bedsheet with holes cut in it for head and arms but a white smock is even better. What you wear underneath it is up to you but the important factors are comfort and freedom of movement. Where pigeon are concerned you will be taking shots from all angles and you must not be hampered.

Many pigeon-shooters wear a mesh face-mask. I am in agreement with them that your face is the main giveaway, the part of your body that they will spot first but I find a mask uncomfortable and never shoot well with one. Certainly it stops the flies from settling on you in the summer months!

There are a number of good portable hides on the market but I have rarely yet shot pigeon anywhere where I have been unable to construct one from foliage, bales or something that is lying around. The main purpose of a hide is to break up the outline of the human body; it does not have to resemble a bush or be realistic. Providing it does not stand out from its background and gives you ample space to shoot from, it does not really matter what your hide looks like. Netting is handy; it can be rolled up and carried in your shooting

Walking round in search of a casual shot at pigeons. (Photo: Lance Smith)

bag and is easily draped over branches or sticks. It is essential that the top of the hide is higher than your crouching or sitting body. That way you will be able to bring your gun up without being deteced by the incoming birds; large bags are made by the decoyer who shoots the birds before they spot him. That way you will average a good ratio of kills to cartridges; if the pigeons are jerking and swerving you will miss an awful lot, lose confidence, and the resulting head killed will be a lot less than had you been properly hidden in the first place.

Gun and cartridges

There is an old belief that the woodpigeon carries a lot of shot and is hard to kill. Indeed, when I was learning to shoot I had it drummed into me by an 'old-stager' that 'you always need No. 4s for pigeons'. Actually No. 7s are ideal *provided you are able to judge range.* As I have already stated I don't like wasting cartridges and I generally take my birds at about thirty yards. Another piece of advice I was once given was that there was such a thickness of feathers on the pigeon's breast that one should always take going-away birds! It doesn't matter how they are flying so long as you hit them fair and square. Always try for a head shot. Lately I have gone back to using No. 5s, not because I found 7s ineffective but simply because I had a surplus of 5 shot, and, as I was killing with them, I stuck to them.

You don't need a magnum to kill pigeons. The heavier the gun, the more cumbersome it will become when the shooting hots up. A lightweight game gun is admirable for the job, particularly when pigeons are coming fast from different directions and you need to snap-shoot. One of the best bags of pigeon I ever made was in the long drought of 1976; I was shooting with my sixteen-bore 'drilling', using an assortment of very old hand-loaded rolled turnover cartridges, a mixture of 4s and 5s. If you can hit the birds don't confuse yourself by studying ballistics.

I have never favoured an over-and-under gun although if it suits you then go ahead. For me, the traditional side-by-side is a compliment to the shooting scene; I was brought up with one and I'll stick to one. When I first started work I saved a pound a week towards having my own gun made. Being a wildfowling enthusiast in those days as well as a rough-shooter, I decided upon a 3-inch magnum with 26-inch barrels. There was a belief still lingering in those days that the longer the barrel, the greater the range, and I had some difficulty in persuading a gunmaker to make my gun to my own specifications. However, the task was completed finally, one of the last guns that the Midland Gun Company made before they closed down. I still have that gun, using it alternately with my lightweight 25-inch game gun and it has served me well for 25 years. Its cost, including case and cleaning equipment and 50 3-inch cartridges, was under £90!

Decoys

I don't intend to become involved in a heated argument over the best kind of decoys to use; shell, whole, flappers, lofters or anything else which some inventive genius has thought up. I have a friend who is an expert on decoying and has made his own decoys. These are full-bodied and about double the size of a live pigeon. They are an exceptional draw, especially when lofted. As he so rightly says, and proved it also with some giant duck decoys, the larger the decoy the easier it is for the birds to see them.

I bought a dozen Max Baker decoys about twenty years ago and have never used anything else. Some of them are repaired with tape, a couple are headless but it doesn't seem to matter. *The art of decoying is to put out your decoys where pigeons are feeding to bring the birds within range of the gun*; it is no good just sticking them out in the open and hoping that they will draw pigeons in, because they won't.

There is much written and talked today about the 'modern' pigeon and how it is more wary, how its habits have changed. I don't dispute this; I believe that the changing face of agriculture has affected the woodie's feeding habits. The increase in oilseed rape fields means that often it can feed in some unapproachable spot, and with acres and acres to choose from it is not interested in a few decoys. Also, it is pursued by the sportsman to such a

Pigeon decoying. (Photo: Lance Smith)

degree these days that its wariness has increased as a result. In the days of the big bags there were more pigeon and far less shooters.

You are suitably clothed and armed, you have your hide and decoys and a scouting expedition in the countryside has led you to a farm where you have permission to shoot. You are eager to go so let us take a quick look at the types of decoying you might encounter.

1. *Laid barley.* Personally I would be very wary of laid barley and I certainly would not allow my dog anywhere near any. Watch to see which patch the pigeons are mostly feeding on, put them off but don't fire a shot until you are set-up and ready. You can't go tramping through growing corn so you are hoping for a site within shooting distance of a boundary hedge which will form part of your hide. Set your decoys out and during the lulls in the shooting prop up your dead birds amongst the artificial ones with a forked stick holding their heads upright. Dead birds are the best decoys of all but make sure you pick up any scattered feathers because these will serve to warn incoming birds.

2. *Oilseed rape.* A difficult one, this. If you chance to find the right spot you might do well, but if your luck is out you will find birds dropping down to feed well out of gunshot and ignoring your decoys.

3. *Brassicas in winter.* In a severe spell of weather pigeons will swarm on anything that shows green through the snow. I recall shooting with a friend in the hard winter of 1962/63 when the pigeons came in regardless. We did not need our white sheets, hide or decoys. You could stand out in the open and shoot them, doing our best to kill them on the wing before they clustered on the sprout tops. It wasn't my idea of sport but the farmer was becoming frantic about the way his crop was being devastated and provided us with the cartridges. The birds themselves were not worth eating anyway.

4. *Bilberries.* During July and August woodpigeons will gorge themselves on this delicious fruit and in large tracts of forest, where there are sometimes extensive clearings that still grow bilberries and heather, the birds will flight in to feed all day. On open moorland a convenient pool or stream is often a good place for the pigeons will feed and then come to slake their thirst.

5. *'Sitty' trees.* In a good acorn year such as 1984 the oak woods offer good sport. Such a wood was the 'Hanging Wood' on my father's small shoot and it was here that the tenant farmer one day made a bag of ninety, just standing amidst the trees, using an old single-barrel 12-bore from which he had sawn off 2 inches of the barrel where it had burst one day!

Disposing of shot pigeons

Woodpigeons make delicious eating but in reality only the breast offers anything in the way of meat. If you skin the breast of your shot bird, lift it upwards, cut through the shoulder joints with a strong pair of kitchen scissors, you are left with a 'pigeon-steak'. These take up little room in your freezer and are delicious eating. In this age of chemical farming I always throw away the innards of any bird or beast I prepare for the table because that is where the bulk of any poisonous residue will be. Which is why I prefer pigeons that have been feeding on either bilberries or acorns.

There is a market for woodpigeons but the price has dropped considerably since those days in the 'seventies when exporters were stockpiling woodies in their deep-freeze warehouses for the continentals. Another 'mountain' was created and demand fell, thankfully, for with 50p per bird being offered greedy shooters were decimating the pigeon population for blood-money. I am a pot-hunter but I do not shoot for money, only to furnish my own larder. Nowadays restaurants will pay around 20p for pigeons. Once despised, the woodpigeon has become a delicacy.

Pigeon breasts are good eating. (Photo: David Cluett)

Legitimate permission to shoot

You are now well satisfied because your efforts have led to several instances of permission to shoot. You have proved yourself reliable and efficient but there is one thing you must check on when permission is granted. *Has the farmer the right to give you permission?*

A farmer has the right to authorise up to three people to shoot vermin on his land even if he is only a tenant, but I have personally known conflict between tenant-farmer and landowner over this, with the sportsman the meat in the sandwich. A farmer has the right to have his crops protected but where the shooting is let an agreement may have been made between the owner of the land and his shooting tenants. Responsibility for crop protection may have been delegated to either a syndicate or their keeper. To save unpleasant-ness at a later date, investigate this, and if there is a gamekeeper, approach him.

In any case always carry your shotgun certificate with you. If the police are called they will demand to see it, and if you have not got it with you then there is the possibility that your gun will be confiscated and held at a police station until you go with your certificate to claim it.

Be prepared and fear nobody.

SHOOTING AND FERRETING RABBITS

It is an offence for a landowner to harbour rabbits on his land and as such permission may be more easily obtained than with woodpigeons. Since myxomatosis rabbit populations seem to fluctuate. They breed prolifically and then comes another outbreak of the disease and reduces them to minimal proportions. But in the meantime a farmer is responsible for controlling them and you might just be lucky.

There is always the chance that the man with ferrets and nets could be given permission in preference to the one with a gun. If you prefer rabbiting to pigeon-shooting then you should learn to manage and work ferrets, for in this way you will double or even treble your bag as opposed to walking rabbits up in rough cover or sitting in wait for them outside a wood on a spring or summer evening.

Ferrets

Ferrets are not the smelly vicious creatures they are reputed to be by the layman. If they are then it is the fault of the owner who has neglected them, neither handled them enough nor cleaned out their hutch regularly. They are affectionate creatures and the sportsman must build up a relationship with them as he does with his dog.

Begin with a pair of ferrets from good stock but *not* a breeding pair. You need to learn how to manage ferrets before becoming involved in breeding. Two jills (females) are better than two hobs (males). Smaller animals are preferable to larger ones because they have more mobility beneath ground.

Living quarters

The hutch should be out of doors, light and airy. The siting should be out of the wind but refrain from choosing a damp sunless place. Preferably buy or make a moveable hutch so that you can alter its position according to weather conditions.

Feeding

A flesh diet is vital to the health of ferrets; they are carnivores and table scraps are no good to them. They prefer their meat as they would kill it in the wild, rabbits in fur, pigeons, etc. in feather. The sportsman should be able to feed his ferrets cheaply by retaining a proportion of his kills for that purpose. Rabbits, pigeons, poultry heads, lights from the butcher's shop can be kept in the freezer so that fresh meat is always on hand.

Ferrets need to be fed twice daily and it is dangerous to overfeed them. I have known an instance where this has happened and the creatures have gorged themselves and died.

At all times there must be fresh water available and a little milk can be given once a day, preferably with the morning feed. My advice is to feed your ferrets an hour or so before working them; a hungry ferret is liable to lie up with a rabbit in a burrow and then you will have to dig it out.

Working ferrets to rabbits

A ferret, like a gundog, has to be trained. A young ferret is always more enthusiastic about a hole that slopes *uphill* and it is best to begin with a hole in a bank. It is always preferable to work it with an experienced ferret so if you know of somebody who has one take yours out with his for its first lesson. Put a line on the older ferret and enter yours with it. If you have to dig your ferrets out don't worry because a young ferret always benefits from being dug out. Try and find a rabbit on that first outing; it sharpens the young ferrets' enthusiasm, and lets them see what it is all about. By tying strips of string at intervals on the line on the jill you will have a fair idea of how far she has gone underground with her companions.

For the second lesson use a deserted warren. Your young ferrets should now begin to work eagerly and they will search diligently for a rabbit. If they emerge into the open, enter them again, and the important thing is to teach them to return to hand eagerly. Avoid boredom; a bored ferred will lose its keenness and will be inclined to wander in deep burrows. An hour is ample for each lesson.

In the early stages it is preferable to net rabbits rather than to shoot them as ferrets need to be introduced to gunfire steadily. Likewise, leave your dog at home; this is another introduction that will have to be done gradually. Let them get used to your dog around the hutch, sit it close by during feeding times.

Only fully experienced ferrets should be used for ratting. A rat is vicious when cornered and, apart from the risk of possible injury or death, you might make your ferrets shy of going below ground.

Equipment

You will need the following equipment before you begin rabbiting in earnest:

1. A good spade for those occasions when you have to dig your ferrets out.
2. A carrying-box for transporting your ferrets. A bag is often stifling, becomes saturated on a wet day and there is little protection for the ferrets if something is dropped on them.
3. Purse-nets for netting rabbits which bolt.
4. A hammer with which to drive in the purse-net pegs.
5. Leather knee-caps. Often the ground is wet and you will spend an awful lot of time on your knees.
6. A rod for probing burrows in an attempt to locate a missing ferret.
7. Muzzles. I am reluctant to use muzzles as a matter of course because if a missing ferret is not found it will be unable to feed and will starve. A muzzle is useful in training, though, and also for putting on an adult jill when searching for lost ferrets so that she does not join them in lying up with their kill.

Check the ground you are going to ferret the day beforehand. Look for entrances to burrows hidden by briars and undergrowth. One overlooked hole could lose you several rabbits. If there are any holes in difficult places, close them up. By doing all this the day beforehand you will avoid disturbing the rabbits below ground on the day; rabbits which are wary are reluctant to bolt and you may well have your ferrets lying up with their kills as a result.

When you begin the assault on the burrows, move as quietly as possible and do not talk whilst fixing your nets. Noise must be kept to a minimum. The moment you have a rabbit in a net, pounce on it at once, despatch it and put the net back in position.

If you are shooting the bolting rabbits then safety is of vital importance.

Guns must be aware of where everybody is in addition to choosing places where they have the maximum vision. Awkward holes should either be blocked up or netted.

Disposal of rabbits

There is a greater demand for rabbits than for pigeons. Most poulterers will buy your rabbits but shop around first because the price fluctuates. Often markets are the best places to take your surplus and you might be lucky and get £1 per head.

Netted or snared rabbits fetch a higher price than shot ones. Presentation is important; they should be gutted neatly and tied by the back legs. They may also be 'legged', a method by which a slit is made in one back leg and the other pushed through it. Rabbits should be delivered to your buyer as soon as possible after killing. In the meantime hang them up in a cool place. There is an old saying that one should only eat rabbits when there is an 'r' in the month, i.e. September to April. This goes back to pre-refrigeration days when it was impossible to store rabbits during the warmer months and also takes into account the breeding season. You will get your best prices for winter rabbits; many people are squeamish about the possibility of eating a doe that has been in kindle, but in all honesty I have not noticed any difference.

And don't forget to offer the farmer who gave you permission a couple of rabbits. He will appreciate the gesture even if he does not accept them and know that you are not just out to get all you can for nothing. Many farmers and gamekeepers feed their rabbits to their dogs, throwing them the carcass in fur. Don't forget to keep one or two back for your ferrets.

If you are seen to be doing a good job keeping the rabbit population in check on a farm it is likely you will always be welcome there and some other shooting may well follow.

Snaring

Snaring is an alternative to shooting or ferreting rabbits but needs considerable practice. Unless there is an infestation of rabbits, though, you must be content to pick up just a few. Also, you must be able to inspect your snares twice a day, not solely on humanitarian grounds but because foxes and buzzards will soon find your catches. Once a fox is aware of a line of rabbit-snares it will use it as an easy source of food.

First you need to establish a line of rabbit 'runs'. Examine them carefully, note where they are coming from and going to. This task will be even easier in snow. When setting snares out in an open field one needs to catch the rabbit on his 'jumps' which are between his footprints, and as such the height of the snare has to be judged very carefully. Only experience will teach you this. However, I have had most of my success setting my snares in the stools of a hedge through which rabbits pass. It saves a lot of time and effort; you do not need to knock in a peg for every snare because invariably there is a trunk handy to tie it to. However, some marker for each snare is necessary otherwise you will waste time searching for snares and doubtless miss the odd one. Count how many you put out and be sure that when you take them up you do not leave one behind. A forgotten snare can cause an awful lot of suffering.

After darkness has fallen is a good time to go round your snares with a torch for rabbits are most active then. Check them again as soon after daylight as possible.

When you purchase new snares they should be buried in the ground for a day or two to remove the smell of newness from them. It also dulls the shininess which might glint and warn an oncoming rabbit.

Don't gut your rabbits near your snares and leave the entrails lying about. This will only encourage foxes and other vermin.

Shooting after dark

The owner or occupier of land is entitled to shoot his rabbits after dark using the headlights of a vehicle. If he authorises you to control his rabbits in this way then that is fine . . . unless local residents complain. I have no knowledge of any court case over legitimate night-shooting but one has to be reasonable and look at it from nearby inhabitants' point-of-view.

I cannot see that the occasional nocturnal rabbit shoot up until, say, 10.30 pm will cause anybody any inconvenience. By 'occasional' I mean about once a month. I know from experience that the first shoot is usually the best; the grazing rabbits are caught unawares and don't know what is going on. Try it a few nights later and it will be a different story; you catch a glimpse of bobbing white tails in the extreme range of the headlights as the coneys bound for the nearest hedgerow. They soon learn that vehicles and lights are associated with guns.

I am not happy shooting from the back of a pick-up truck or Land Rover unless I am the sole gun, operating just with a driver, the two of us taking it in turns to drive and shoot. Guns and vehicles are a dangerous combination. A skid or a bump and a gun is likely to be discharged.

If you are really determined to shoot rabbits after dark then the best way is to go on foot, taking a companion with you to shine a strong lamp. This way is safer and offers less disturbance. My main objection to night-shooting is that if you disturb a covey of partridge it will fly blind and a fence could decimate half the birds. Gunfire after dark is not conducive to good game preservation. The less wildlife is disturbed, the better.

General vermin-control

As a result of your efforts at either pigeon or rabbit control you *could* just find yourself in a position that would be the envy of all other luckless searchers for shooting. The farmer, or syndicate, or whoever has the shooting rights over which you have been rabbiting and pigeon-shooting, asks you if you would be interested in doing some part-time gamekeeping. They want to increase the potential of the shoot, rear a few birds and keep the vermin down but they have not the time to do it themselves. So you find yourself in the role of part-time keeper, all the vermin shooting you want, and in return you have to rear a few pheasants. And perhaps your perk will be an invitation to shoot with them during the season.

So far we have covered all the major duties that will be expected of you but you will do well to study the forthcoming chapters on duck flight-pond management, and their construction if there is not an available pool on your land, and also the chapter on poachers for you are likely to meet up with them on a shoot of any size these days.

But, in the meantime, for the benefit of anyone who has not been able to acquire a small shoot of his own, cannot afford to join a syndicate, and all his requests for vermin-shooting have been turned down, we shall consider the prospect of some coastal wildfowling.

CHAPTER SEVEN

Coastal Wildfowling

Coastal wildfowling is the toughest, most demanding of all shotgun sports. It sorts out the ardent sportsman from the casual shot, entails hours spent in lonely places at the mercy of the elements with, all too often, very little in the bag to show for one's efforts. Yet you are likely to contract a condition known as 'goose fever', the irresistible call of the marshes which will lure you back time after time. Wildfowling is something special and I shall do my utmost to impart some of that atmosphere to you in the ensuing chapter.

The face of wildfowling has changed over the last few years. With new legislation included in the Wildlife and Countryside Act, 1981, and the introduction of SSSIs, the wildfowler has had a raw deal and is justifiably incensed by the new restrictions imposed upon him.

Wildfowling was once free shooting for anyone within travelling distance of the coast as the land below high-water mark was the property of the Crown and, as such, anybody was entitled to shoot there. The main goose wintering grounds of the British Isles were the Solway Firth and the Wash. And it was on the Solway where I began my wildfowling career.

I shot my first goose on the merse at Brow Well, and proved the worth of my new magnum with its 26-inch barrels that sunny Monday morning. On the Friday I shot another. Both were magnificent greylags and it was a holiday to remember. Thereafter, for fifteen years I made that annual trek up to south-west Scotland but I didn't kill a lot of geese. Times were changing, the era of the 'marsh cowboy' had begun, that inexplicable armed species whose object is to fire as many shots as possible at skeins of geese which have learned to fly higher and higher. It is a pointless moronic exercise, for at best they prick birds; most of the time the geese are three or four gunshots high. I deplore this wild shooting for it only serves to spoil the sport for everybody else and brings shooting into disrepute. Every so often an unlucky goose planes down and there is a mad stampede to claim it, nobody knows who has shot it but most of them know very well that *they* haven't; sometimes they come to blows, there are heated arguments and the true wildfowler walks off in disgust.

*Geese flighting over
Criffel on the
Solway Firth.
(Artist: Calvin
Williams)*

My only regret is that I persevered with the Solway for so long. I shot my last goose on the merse in 1969 but continued fowling there until 1972. During the last three years I never fired a shot at geese; they were specks in the sky, night and morning, and even their magical calling was drowned by a barrage of fire.

If everybody held their fire and only shot at geese that were within range then everybody would get geese from time to time. Instead there is this mad desperation to loose off shots so nobody shoots any. This unwelcome element of shooters have no knowledge of wildfowl and there is no logic in their behaviour. For some reason they want to take a goose home whether or not it has fallen to their gun. Perhaps it is a trophy to brag to their friends about but whatever their reason, if there is one, they can know no satisfaction. Once there were some dead geese stolen from the game cellar in one of the wildfowling hotels, an act which is more deplorable than mere theft. A party

A skein of whitefronted geese. (Photo: Calvin Williams)

of shooters who had outwitted both the geese and the hooligans went home gooseless as a result.

In between my Solway visits I was also shooting on the Wash. This was in the days of the late Kenzie Thorpe, the famous wildfowler, poacher and TV personality in his latter years. When Kenzie accompanied you as guide, woe betide you if you took a long shot, showed yourself too soon or spoiled the sport in any other way. His forays were not for the faint-hearted; you went out on to the mud to shoot geese and more often than not you came back with some.

The Wash is a completely different proposition from the Solway. Whilst the latter has dangerous tides and quicksands, on the Solway there are miles of firm grassy merse where you can walk safely in ordinary knee-length wellington boots. By contrast the Wash is thick mud with deep creeks that can fill with the incoming tide and cut you off from the sea wall. The cover is sparse, you crouch in muddy creeks with your waders sinking in all the time and learn to shoot from a variety of different, uncomfortable positions.

The main quarry here are pinkfeet geese which migrate from Spitzbergen to use it as a wintering ground. On my lounge wall hangs one of Kenzie's distinctive paintings that captures the very atmosphere of those windswept marshes. A sunset scene with skein after skein of geese flighting back from their feeding grounds across Shep White's. Sadly, it isn't like that now.

The geese moved up to the Wash from Wells-next-the-Sea between the two wars. The Wells gunners had bombarded them night and morning but when selfish shooters began digging-in out on the mud where the birds roosted, and blasting them on moonlight nights, the pinkfeet had had enough. Gradually they filtered away, and began to use the mudflats of the Wash. From 1950 onwards there was a vast increase in the number of wildfowlers on these marshes. The war and petrol rationing were a thing of the past, society was more affluent and more and more people began to take up shooting. If you had a car and a gun, and were within motoring distance of Sutton Bridge, then there was nothing to stop you shooting on the Wash every day of the week if you wanted to. By 1960 wildfowling guides were fully booked for most of the season. If you were not familiar with the marshes you needed a guide. Most of them charged ten shillings per flight; Kenzie cost a pound and was well worth every penny of it.

But once again the geese were being harassed, not by the guides and their parties but by those who lined the sea wall and thought that they had had their money's worth on morning or evening flight if they got through a couple of boxes of cartridges. As a result less and less geese began returning each autumn. They dispersed, mostly up as far as Skegness; some returned to Wells but not in any great numbers.

I feel that generally wildfowling clubs came on the scene too late. Whilst clubs have existed since the early part of this century it was only comparatively recently that they began to rent stretches of saltings and foreshore; they privatised them yet secured the sport for their members and charged visitors a nominal daily or weekly fee to shoot there. They made every effort to reduce the numbers of indiscriminate shooters but that is a problem which will never totally be resolved.

Habitats were also changing to the detriment of wildfowl. Marshland was being reclaimed and modern agriculture was reducing the traditional inland feeding grounds of the wild goose. Whilst nature reserves are beneficial to the wildfowl, conservation and shooting are linked, a fact which some organisations are unable to accept even today. The fowler was up against restrictions, his traditional shooting grounds being slowly whittled away. Large acreages of marshland were being purchased as sanctuaries where no shooting was allowed. It was the thin end of the wedge, something which we shall look at in more detail in the final chapter of this book.

But suffice to say that no longer is there ample free fowling along the shorelines of Great Britain. Nevertheless, there is still some excellent wild-fowling to be had and we must look at this in an objective way and equip ourselves suitably so that we can conduct ourselves properly in a sport that is constantly under the microscope of the critical conservationists and those who would wish it banned altogether.

The quarry

The foremost task is to be able to identify one's quarry. This is of vital importance on the foreshore where, during a morning or evening flight, duck and geese which are protected species may fly within gunshot. If in doubt, don't shoot and take steps to identify the species which mystified you. You may shoot the following birds but please also refer to the shooting seasons given earlier in this book for when they may be killed:

Coot	Mallard
Tufted Duck	Moorhen
Gadwall	Pintail
Goldeneye	Golden Plover
Canada Goose	Pochard
Greylag Goose	Shoveler
Pinkfooted Goose	Common Snipe
White-fronted Goose	Teal
(in England and Wales only)	Wigeon

Protected species

All other duck, geese and wading birds except those mentioned above are protected but we should look at one or two species which were once the legitimate quarry of the fowler and have been taken from him.

Barnacle goose. A few years prior to my first Solway visit the barnacle goose was one that figured largely in the fowler's bag. A predominantly black, white and grey goose, the majority of the winter migratory flock is to be seen on the Caerlaverock Nature Reserve in Scotland. Mostly they graze the grass on the reserve there and are to be frequently seen. Their call is unmistakable, a canine-like yapping which the layman could be forgiven for mistaking for a pack of hounds in the distance. They rarely venture far inland and once seen are unlikely to be confused with other geese. I have heard conflicting comments on their edibility but I am sure that the genuine fowlers of years gone by would not have shot them unless they were acceptable as a table bird.

The barnacle was put on the protected list in 1954. In 1945 the wintering population on the Solway had dropped to an alarming 300 birds, but in fact the numbers had already begun to increase before the protection act was in force. Nowadays the flock is counted in its thousands but the species still remains protected by law except in cetain northern areas during the month of April when the geese present a threat to growing crops, particularly grazing areas which are needed for livestock. A dispensation allows them to be culled there yet the wildfowler, who would do this admirably during the shooting season, is forbidden to kill them.

Greylag goose. (Photo: Calvin Williams)

Greylag goose: the main quarry of the fowler. (Photo: Lance Smith)

The brent goose. Grey and black geese, they are seldom found far from the sea. In recent years their numbers have increased greatly but they still remain protected.

Curlew. This long-billed wading bird with the mournful warbling cry is familiar to most people. During the summer months it is seen inland on moors where it breeds before returning to the mudflats in mid-August. Curlew are a common sight, graceful fliers that swerve and jink at the first sign of danger, offering the most sporting of shots. In the early part of the season they are delicious eating with plenty of meat on them. In no way have their numbers been in danger of diminishing, indeed quite the reverse. Obscure reasons were given for protecting them, even though a minimal number are shot by fowlers. In spite of the efforts of BASC the decision was not reversed and the fight still goes on to get them reinstated as a sporting quarry. The genuine fowler has been deprived of a worthy quarry, together with the redshank and all other wading species except the common snipe.

BASIC ADVICE FOR THE BEGINNER

Clothing

Whatever you wear it must blend with your surroundings, be waterproof and warm, and allow maximum mobility for of all the shotgun sports you will not find another where you are required to shoot from almost every posture outside a yoga manual, your feet entrenched in sucking mud and your fingers numbed by cold. Waders are a must because you will often have to cross deep creeks and they are also useful for kneeling in. Your hat needs to fit your head snugly because most of the time you will be out in strong winds and again I would advocate the deerstalker with the flaps pulled down over your ears. Always take a game-bag because the less you are encumbered by carrying things, the better.

Buy, and learn to use, a reliable compass

On marshland sea mists can come down in a few minutes, obscuring the landscape and otherwise familiar landmarks. The fowler without a compass can easily find himself walking seawards and discover his mistake when it is too late. The tides have claimed several wildfowlers' lives, lives that might have been saved with the aid of a compass. But do learn to read it and take a reading before setting out.

Guns and cartridges

This is one instance where I am not going to advocate a lightweight game gun and No. 7s! Out on the marshes you will be shooting at maximum ranges (*not out of range*) where you need to hit hard and the fewer runners, the better. Basically you need a good sound 3-inch magnum, fully choked in both barrels. The salt air will play havoc with a good gun and even with a modest one you need to clean it on your return home, the moment you have dried and fed your dog.

Don't use a shot size smaller than No. 4, and for geese use 3s, 1s or BBs; nothing larger because what you gain in penetration you lose in pattern. At 40 yards No. 3s will crumple up a goose without any trouble.

Accessories

Accessories are the choice of the individual – he has the job of carrying them! A *goose call* is useful *if* you know how to use one; if you don't, either practise or forget it. A call not used properly will have just the reverse effect.

Likewise decoys can sometimes make all the difference between a good or mediocre bag but only take them out when you have a specific decoying destination in mind. The less you carry around with you, the better.

Tides

Tides are the basis of sport; *they can also drown you if you get caught out by them.* As well as your compass you need a tide-table. You must be aware of when the tides ebb and flow and bear in mind that strong winds can make a difference of up to an hour. It isn't just a question of retreating before an incoming tide, it is the creeks behind you which are the danger. The one you crossed on the way out had less than a foot of water in it; it could be seven or eight feet deep when you get back to it, for the creeks will fill up long before the tide covers the saltmarshes.

Don't be tempted to stay on an extra ten minutes because the duck are flighting well. All the duck on the marsh aren't worth risking your life for.

Tides will determine a daytime flight of duck. They will push the birds off sandbanks or mudflats and if you are in the right position you could enjoy sport equivalent to dawn or dusk flights. But you need to be exceptionally well hidden for you do not have the cloak of darkness as a hide. A length of camouflage netting rolled up in your shooting bag can be very handy for tide-flighting.

Likewise you must learn to judge range accurately in wide open spaces where there are no specific landmarks such as trees or hedges. There is an old maxim that says if you can blot out a bird with your barrels then it's out of range. Only experience will teach you, but better to under-estimate range in the early stages than to over-estimate it.

Geese

Geese will fly out to fields to feed at daybreak, or soon after, and return in the evening. But adverse weather conditions can upset their routine. In thick fog they will often fly up and down the edge of the marsh trying to find their bearings, and if you are lucky you could enjoy good sport at very shootable birds because they will not be high. Strong gales will also force them to fly low.

A full moon will alter their feeding pattern and sometimes they will stop out in the fields all night. They are also likely to fly around the marsh in the moonlight on short forays and this is when decoys in conjunction with a call will bring them in to you.

Night-shooting can be good sport and is perfectly harmless to the environment on coastal marshes. There was a move made to ban it during the compiling of the Wildlife and Countryside Act but fortunately this failed. A full moon is traditionally the time when the experienced fowler likes to be out and about, not solely to bag a goose or a duck but to enjoy the sheer splendour of a majestic lonely world that is still the domain of nature.

Duck

Duck are greedy birds and spend their lives searching for food. On the coast they rest out on the mud by day and flight inland at night. The marsh gunner will meet up with mallard, teal, wigeon, pintail, gadwall, goldeneye, pochard and shoveler and must learn to identify each species in the half-light. When traversing the marsh in daylight examine all flashes of water for signs of preening feathers and droppings. If these are in evidence, return well before dark and establish a hide, even put a few decoys on the water. If there is absolutely no cover available then you may have to lie on your back with a piece of camouflage-netting draped over you. Personal comfort is something which you will have to disregard if you are to enter into the true spirit of wildfowling.

Where duck are to be found in numbers, don't be greedy. One move I did welcome, and I am sure most other true sportsmen did also, was the restrictions on automatic shotguns by recent legislation. My motto has always been, 'If you can't hit them with two barrels, they deserve to get away, and two barrels are enough for anybody.' In the past years I have witnessed fowlers blazing away at wigeon with automatics and this is where sport becomes greed. Automatics now have to be 'blanked off' to take no more than three cartridges, and rightly so.

Canada geese

Canada geese have multiplied to pest proportions in many parts of Great Britain and it is an offence to rear these birds for releasing into the wild. Almost everybody, whether they live in rural or urban areas, are familiar with the large black and white goose. There are flocks of them on numerous lakes and parks, some even taking bread from you if you go to feed them. But away from these domesticated environments the Canada is as wild as any wild goose and offers good sport. In my own opinion is is the best of all geese on the table.

There is no mistaking its loud trumpeting call. Flocks of Canadas often follow the pattern of grey geese in the early part of the season, roosting on the mudflats by night and flighting out to the fields or lakes to feed during the daylight hours. Don't spurn the chance to shoot one, they are legitimate quarry and a worthy prize.

How to find wildfowling

Wildfowling is possibly the easest form of all shooting to locate. However, the matter needs to be approached systematically and once again the importance of BASC membership is demonstrated.

At the time of writing this chapter a list of wildfowling clubs which issue visitors' permits appeared in the columns of the *Shooting Times*, compiled by

Canada goose: an agricultural pest but a worthy quarry. (Photo: Lance Smith)

the BASC. This is a short directory of permit-issuing officers who can be approached with a view to obtaining shooting either by the day or the week. It is stressed, however, that BASC membership cards must be enclosed with all applications. This is by no means a complete list and if the area one wishes to shoot is not given then the Association should be contacted to see if wildfowling is obtainable on a particular marsh.

Permits can cost up to £5 per day or £20 a week, which is cheap shooting when one considers the cost of pigeon or vermin shooting inland! Most clubs allocate a maximum number of permits per week in order that their marshes are not overcrowded or over-shot. There will also be certain regulations which must be adhered to, and a violation of these will result in the offending member having his permit withdrawn and in all probability being banned by the club for future seasons.

A visitor is not guaranteed sport; all he gets in return for his money is the right to shoot on a particular stretch of foreshore at a designated time. The rest is up to him; nobody, I am sure, will begrudge him that extra bit of luck which puts a few duck or geese in the bag.

Severe weather

Hard weather is the time when fowling is at its best and with the advent of Christmas the sport should be at its peak. However, the sportsman must not

Canada goose: a worthy quarry. (Photo: Lance Smith)

A Solway wildfowler's bag. (Photo: Calvin Williams)

use intense spells of severe climatic conditions to make large bags. Self-restraint is the hallmark of the true fowler.

In recent years the government has introduced bans on wildfowling during hard winters. Commendable as this may be, a 'blanket' ban on shooting is short-sighted. Perhaps the north of the country is in the grip of arctic weather whilst further south it is relatively mild and the fowl are not short of food. It is unfair in this case when southerners are included in the ban.

Monitor weather conditions carefully on the week prior to your wildfowling trip. Possibly the best forecast to watch is the BBC's Sunday lunchtime forecast for farmers and growers when a rundown of the weather for the following week is given. I have found this to be reasonably accurate overall, and in any case one gets a good idea of what might be looming ahead. It is pointless to make a 300-mile journey if a fowling ban is imminent and the Met. Office say there will be no let-up in the snow and ice.

Accommodation

Good accommodation can either make or spoil a wildfowling trip. There are advertisements for such most weeks in the sporting press, ranging from self-catering cottages, chalets and caravans, to bed-and-breakfast establishments or good hotels who are glad of the shooting season once the conventional tourist trade is over. Weigh them all up carefully and if in doubt contact the

Tourist Information Office of the town nearest to the foreshore where you intend to shoot.

Decide what you want and what you can afford; cost your trip before fixing accommodation. Also take into account how much time you can afford in the preparation of meals. If you can persuade your wife to accompany you then that is half the battle and you need worry no more, but spare a thought for her during those long hours when you will be out on the marshes, morning and evening flights and perhaps a tide-flight as well. What will she do with herself? If the cottage is in a remote area then it will not be much fun for her being stranded there all day because you have used the car to travel to the marsh. But if the cottage is within walking distance of the saltings then you can leave her the car and she can go into town, maybe do some sight-seeing as well. All these factors must be taken into consideration if the holiday is to be a success.

Wildfowling is a physically demanding sport and at the end of the day when you return to your digs, cold and wet, the prospect of lighting a fire and cooking a meal is a daunting one. Short cuts, junk convenience foods will not enhance your holiday, neither will it benefit you during a week when you are using up a lot of energy.

If you can afford it, hotels or guest-houses *catering specifically for wildfowlers* are the best bet. Check on their facilities beforehand, though. You will need warm, dry kennelling for your dog, somewhere to dry your wet clothing and clean your gun, a safe place to hang that coveted goose if you shoot one. Hoteliers seeking to cash in on a winter trade without providing the necessary facilities will be in for a rude awakening; guests will tramp in wet and muddy from the marsh, and the hotel will soon lose its smart summer appearance. If they advertise for wildfowling guests then they have to be able to cope with all that goes with the sport.

Mealtimes should be flexible. No fowler wants to break off from a promising evening flight because he has to be back in the dining-room by 6 pm. Neither does he want to leave the marsh early after morning-flight when there are still geese out on the mudflats. Sometimes, particularly on a dull, damp morning, wild geese do not hurry to flight out to their feeding grounds.

You will need to be in position on the marsh before it gets light; if you arrive late not only will you spoil the sport for others but the best positions will be occupied. Thus you will need a very early cup of tea and a piece of toast long before the rest of the hotel is awake. Most hotels are co-operative over this small matter. They allow guests to go into the kitchen and make themselves a snack before going out or else provide flasks and biscuits. If a hotel advertises 'wildfowling accommodation' then you expect the full treatment.

Some of the larger coastal hotels depend upon wildfowling for the bulk of their winter trade. Here you can expect a heated outhouse of some kind for the purpose of drying wet clothing, cleaning your gun and somewhere comfortable for your dog. In addition to this they often provide a guide for the marshes and inland rough-shooting for the enjoyment of guests between morning and evening flights.

Guides

We have already mentioned the professional guide who earns his living by taking shooters out. The hotels are often competing against him and as such the man in question needs to know both the sport and the layout of the saltmarsh. A bad guide is worse than no guide at all.

It is not simply a case of taking a party out twice daily, positioning them along the sea wall and collecting them after the flight is over. The guide must study the birds, check where they are feeding, determine which flight-line is the most likely to provide some sport. If he is paid by the hotel and does a good job, then, like a gamekeeper, he is entitled to a tip. But don't waste a pound on somebody who obviously has little interest or idea, and takes you out to the same gooseless place morning and night. Forget him and do your own reconnaissance.

Rough-shoots

Some hotels rent considerable acreages of rough-shooting for the enjoyment of their guests. But in the case of wildfowling establishments these shoots are an extra and should not be relied upon to provide sport throughout your holiday. They will be shot week-in, week-out, from October through to the end of January; the early season guests will get what birds are there, for the rest it will just be a walk out with the chance of a shot at either pigeons or rabbits. Unless birds have been reared and shoots are reserved for specific dates, then be wary of paying more than a nominal daily fee for this type of 'fill-in' shooting.

Inland goose-shooting

One frequently sees accommodation offering 'wildfowling and inland goose-shooting'. At the outset you want to know what you are getting for your money. 'Wildfowling' means that the place in question is situated within

A mixed bag at the end of a successful day. (Photo: Calvin Williams)

motoring distance of the foreshore. How far? Do they provide a guide or, if not, can they recommend one? Foreshore shooting is your priority; inland geese can be a bonus providing you are not greedy and out to take a carload of geese home. The chances are that you won't but the shooting of grey geese over decoys on the fields inland can offer some memorable sport and should be given a try. Beware of being exploited, though; the situation is on a parallel with the £25 per day pigeon-shooting. You should only pay if there is a reasonable chance of seeing geese. A look at the ground in question will soon tell you whether or not the geese are feeding there. If they are, their droppings will be very much in evidence. Even the raw novice cannot overlook them.

Geese are decoyed fairly easily provided: a. you are well camouflaged; b. your decoys are set out properly, heads into the wind and look realistic; c. the field has not been overshot. Even then there is no guarantee that the birds will show up soon after daybreak.

The field may be grass, recently harvested potatoes with tops and a few tubers till lying about, perhaps carrots. If the droppings are there then the geese have certainly been using it.

The most difficult factor is bringing the geese within range of your gun on a large field, which is why you need decoys. All too often the birds alight in the centre and remain feeding there. They are wary, they like places which allow them plenty of vision. If they do follow this pattern and you enjoy all the thrills of a good stalk then you will earn your bird. The chase will entail a belly-crawl down a hedge or muddy ditch, *with the wind blowing from the geese to you*. Every so often you will risk a discreet peep to check on the geese; if they have stopped feeding and their heads are erect, then they have sensed danger and any second they will be on the wing. If this happens before you are within effective killing range, then let them go and try again tomorrow. A long-range shot will only result in a pricked and lost bird and you will have sacrificed another chance.

If everything goes according to plan then don't go for a big bag. Remember, you are not allowed to sell dead geese so if you come home with a lot what are you going to do with them? One fresh for the table, three or four in the freezer, and how many friends have you who would *really* appreciate a goose in feather as a present? Not many, I suspect. So bear that in mind if you happen on a good flight.

A few years ago a friend and I decided to give the Solway another try after so many years' absence. We were keen to try our hand at shooting geese inland so I began to make a few enquiries. Shooting geese over decoys would cost £30 per flight! To me there is no goose-flight worth that much. Further searching led us back to an old colleague who said he would be able to 'fix us up with something which would not cost more than a tip for the keeper'. Sure enough he did, but this transpired to be flighting geese off an inland loch.

The weather was exceedingly mild and spring-like for January, and a light pullover was sufficient for morning flight. My friend, who is an exceptional wildfowler and a perfectionist at most things he undertakes, loads all his own cartridges. Alphamax 3s were good enough for me but he persuaded me to try some of his home-loaded $1^5/8$ oz No. 1s. I compromised; an Alphamax in the right barrel, Calvin's 'special' in the left.

On the Monday morning the geese went off at the opposite end of the loch, but on the Tuesday a couple of skeins headed towards us. We were standing behind a row of straggling hawthorns, the only cover available. The first skein was Calvin's and he brought off a neat right and left. Then it was my turn, those greylags no more than thirty yards up, just like they used to be in the old days at Brow Well. My first bird folded up neatly and thumped on to the grass, stone dead. I swung on the second, pulled. The awaited report never came; instead there was an ominous click. Calvin's cartridge had misfired!

Back in the hotel gunroom we held an 'inquest' into that frustrating misfire. It appeared that my strikers barely dented the percussion caps of the home-loads yet were true every time on the mass-produced ammunition. A right and left that might have been but wasn't, and as it turned out that was the only goose I shot in those few days. So my family enjoyed a fresh greylag on my return home and that was that. My self-imposed bag limit of ten was never reached.

Wildfowling vehicles

Having the right vehicle for the job is not so important to the wildfowler as having the right gun and cartridges, for with the commercialisation of fowling there are often hard roads right down to the sea wall and sometimes even a suitable place to park. But if you go wildfowling in the dead of winter, those weeks following Christmas, a four-wheel drive vehicle can be an advantage.

The Land Rover is able to cope with most tracts of rough ground and a foot of snow, whereas the more sophisticated vehicles, designed for comfort and normal on-road use as well, provide that extra stability when required, such as a light fall of snow or icy roads.

Nowadays the wildfowler has a wide choice of four-wheel-drive vehicles: Subaru and Land Rover. (Photo: Lance Smith)

Shooting on Caerlaverock

The Caerlaverock National Reserve was formed in 1957. It was a valuable site for a reserve because of the fact that it was an established wintering ground of barnacle geese which, as has been stated earlier, had dwindled to a mere 300 birds in this area at that time. The land was owned by the Duke of Norfolk who agreed to lease it, rent free, as a nature reserve. WAGBI (now BASC) were also at this time interested in forming a sanctuary to protect roosting geese on Blackshaw Bank, the sands adjoining Caerlaverock merse.

The result was a National Nature Reserve at Caerlaverock, comprising something in the region of 1500 acres of grazing merse and 12,000 acres of Blackshaw Bank.

Today we have a prime example of shooting and conservation on Caerlaverock. A wildfowling area was designated, fenced off from the reserve and clearly marked on a map, and a permit scheme was introduced whereby a maximum number of fowlers were allowed on the merse at one time. Patrolling wardens keep a strict eye on proceedings and those who err are likely to be prosecuted and/or have their permits confiscated. Locals can obtain a season permit, visitors on a weekly basis.

The system works in that applications for permits are invited, in writing, from July onwards and are granted on a first-come, first-served basis. Therefore it is necessary to apply early to be sure of shooting on Caerlaverock at the time of your choice.

The permit enables you to:

1. Shoot on the area designated for wildfowling on the map enclosed with your permit, and from the creeks draining through it, between the hours of one hour before sunrise to 10 am, and from 3.30 pm to one hour after sunset. You may use a shotgun not larger than an 8-bore for ducks, geese and other wildfowl in accordance with the Wildlife and Countryside Act, 1981.

2. You may use your dog for the purpose of retrieving.

3. You may also use decoys.

There is no charge for a permit and those wishing to apply should write to:

> The Issuing Officer, Caerlaverock Panel,
> The Nature Conservancy Council,
> The Castle, Loch Lomond Park,
> Balloch, Dunbartonshire G83 8LX.

I never embarked upon a Solway wildfowling trip unless I had a permit to shoot on Caerlaverock as well as the marshes leased by the Solway Wildfowlers' Association. Indeed, Caerlaverock was the first merse I ever set foot on in south-west Scotland.

Caerlaverock reminds me of walking on my lawn at home, short well-grazed turf, except that it is intersected by a maze of shallow creeks and flashes, most of which have firm bottoms and are easily waded. In the early part of the season these shallow pools are frequented by wigeon and teal and one needs to spend a few hours' reconnaissance in order to find out which of the pools the birds are using. There is little or no cover and this is one of the places where you may have to shoot from a lying-down position under cover of a length of camouflage netting.

It is a majestic place with Criffel, the highest mountain in south-west Scotland, in the background. Whether you find any sport or not, a visit to

Caerlaverock will be an unforgettable experience. It will whet your appetite for the sport and undoubtedly give you a bout of 'goose fever'.

The future of wildfowling

Of all shotgun sports, wildfowling is the most vulnerable from legislation. I feel that the genuine fowler is too often made the scapegoat, the lamb cast to the hungry lions to appease them. It need not be so; BASC is working tirelessly on behalf of the wildfowler to secure his sport and in spite of the change of name it is still *your* association. Yet you must not sit back and let your association fight your battles. Let your voice be heard; when outrageous and grossly inaccurate statements are made by the media, write and give the *true* facts. The man in the street knows little or nothing of the sport and will be influenced by what he reads. Make sure the correct facts are put before him. Do not be afraid to lobby your MP. When issues are at stake, write to him, make sure he understands those issues properly as well as your own point of view.

Finding shooting or wildfowling is only half the battle. You have to do your part to secure its future.

CHAPTER EIGHT

Inland Duck Shooting

Often the shooting rights of a small pool may be easier to secure than the farmland adjoining it. This was my own experience during the few years after leaving school, those halcyon days when I shot rabbits for pocket money with my first 12-bore and the prospect of coming to terms with wild duck fired my imagination. I read with envy every shooting book I could get my hands on and was thrilled by the romance of pre-World War I Wells-next-the-Sea and Bill Powell's Solway exploits. But I lived in the heart of the Midlands, the furthest point from all foreshores, and, with no means of transport of my own, one rather inconspicuous reed-fringed pond situated a mere fifty yards from a road became my 'fowling ground'.

The shooting around it was let, so why did the tenant not bother with this flight-pond and was quite happy for me to shoot it whenever I wished so long as I did not forage further afield? Simply because it was a small, overgrown patch of water that merely served as a cattle-drink in hot weather. Nobody could envisage duck using it; perhaps the odd one might flight in there from time to time, and if it did then I was more than welcome to it. Whatever happened, whether it was shot or not, it would not affect the game-shooting. The farmer would not even accept a fiver in rent for it; I pressed him but he refused saying he could not take money under false pretences!

My first task was to try and clear the algae from the surface. I constructed a home-made 'drag' but it didn't work. Eventually it sank. I have learned since that algae on a pool does not act to the detriment of duck-shooting. So I cleared some of the surrounding reeds and opened the water area up to about twenty-five yards by ten yards. Then I began to feed the shallows.

That was in the days when combine-harvesters sorted and bagged weed-seeds, chaff and any other rubbish. Much of it was waste that the duck would not eat but I tipped it all in the water. I discovered then that moorhens were eating the majority of the corn so I culled them. Incidentally, moorhens are good eating, rather like pheasant in flavour. They have to be skinned rather than plucked, probably the reason why they are ignored by the sportsman, although they are on the quarry list.

My feeding also attracted rats. I trapped a number with an old cage-trap situated on the water's edge, and by the time 12 August arrived (the opening date for wildfowl shooting in those days) my optimism was running high. For a month I did not see or hear a duck and I began to think that the farmer and the shooting tenant were right after all, that I was wasting my time.

Then, towards the end of September, a pair of mallard showed up one evening and I dropped one with my old single-barrel. Another lull; in October I shot three more. But it was late November before I really enjoyed any worthwhile sport and this began when teal started using the pool. I discovered that this pond was a favoured haunt of teal, the smallest of the duck species which offer superb sport and delicious eating. I finished the season with twenty duck and was more than satisfied. The farmer smiled, told me to carry on next season. In his opinion teal were not worth powder and shot and if I was happy then that was all right by him.

I shot that pool for ten years until eventually the farm was sold and the new owner, a keen shooting man, recognised the true potential of that tiny patch of water. My record season was 70 duck, 50 teal and 20 mallard, and I shot the last bird on the closing evening of the season.

Since then I have learned to recognise the potential of small, seemingly useless overgrown ponds, even those situated close to a road. Remember, by law you have to be 50 feet from the centre of a carriageway when shooting; this is a minimal distance and there are few pools where one cannot legally shoot simply by standing on the furthest side from the road. Often duck are used to passing vehicles and take no notice of traffic. There is a vast potential of untapped duck-shooting in such pools the length and breadth of Great Britain.

Looking for a small pool

Again it is a motorised foray around the countryside in the same way that you have searched for other types of shooting. Concentrate on rural lanes, drive slowly and stop frequently. Often such pools are hidden behind hedges, even those mutilated by flail-cutters, and you will pass several without noticing them. Again you need to convince farmers of your integrity. In all probability they will think you are crazy wanting to rent the shooting of some pond which they have often considered filling in; you must assure them that you will not shoot game and that you are prepared to do your bit towards vermin-control. If there is a shooting tenant then he will have to be consulted. He may not like the idea of anybody else shooting on the land even though he considers the pond useless. And, of course, once you have developed the flight pond he might decide to capitalise on your hard work but this is a risk which you will have to take.

The secret of your success lies in the greediness of mallard. They spend

Only a small pond, but with the right management it will attract duck.
(Photo: Lance Smith)

their lives searching for food and once it is readily available somewhere they will flight in to feed regardless of the size of the water. On very small pools duck will come at dusk, feed ravenously on whatever you have fed the shallows with, and then fly off to larger areas of water.

There is just such a pond within a hundred yards of my home. Indeed, only the closest inspection would identify it as a pond! Once it had a clay bottom and never dried up but for some reason the water level has dropped and it is now no more than a miniature marsh with grass and reeds growing in it. Yet it pulls the ducks.

This pond is, in fact, a quarter of an acre of genuine common land, principally for the inhabitants of Black Hill to water their livestock. Out of three dwellings only ourselves qualify for this. Likewise I am entitled to shoot there, as is anybody else who wishes to do so but in a remote area such as this that is unlikely. I can see it from my study window; mallard circle over my garden before planing down on to this squelchy patch.

Some time ago I realised its potential and planted up its perimeter with a mixture of conifer, silver birch and rowan trees to provide a future screen from the road. Should I lose one of my rented pools a short distance away then this will be its replacement. In the meantime I am content to allow the duck to get used to feeding there.

A much overgrown roadside pool but the author shoots duck here.
(Photo: Lance Smith)

Such places require only the right management to turn them into worth-while flight-ponds.

Improving a neglected pond

If you are lucky enough to obtain permission to shoot some neglected pond then you must also establish with the farmer that it will be necessary for you to improve it. First, is there sufficent cover round the pool? Duck like to enjoy a degree of privacy whilst at the same time overhanging trees must not impede their comings and goings. Conifers, willows and silver-birch are all fast-growing trees which will provide the necessary cover within a few years, and often one can obtain permission to dig up self-set saplings from wood-lands. To remove seedlings without permission will render one liable to prosecution as it contravenes the Wildlife and Countryside Act, 1981. Choose trees that are roughly three feet high. This means they have a good start; any larger will be rocked by strong winds which will loosen their roots before they have had a chance to root properly and they will die. Plant sparingly for seedlings grow into large trees and you might end up screening your pond in years to come. At deep dusk circling duck must be able to see the water; if it is hidden by shadows they will not and will go elsewhere.

Problems can arise where a pool is completely in the open and yet planting would be a waste of time because the farmer's livestock would only graze your new trees. If he is willing for you to erect a barbed-wire fence then that is the solution to protect your trees (you need three strands to keep out sheep effectively) but in most cases the pool is regarded as a valuable water supply for his animals.

You will not be able to screen the pool then but you can certainly plant some reeds to provide cover for duck. Hides will be your problem for anything you construct of branches or bales will soon be demolished or eaten by the cattle. The answer is to make a hide from pallets. Wooden pallets are generally easily obtainable; haulage firms discard those which are damaged. Four large ones will make a hide large enough for one person. Knock in four stout fencing stakes, run some barbed-wire round them to keep inquisitive cattle and sheep at bay and then lash your pallets securely together, leaving one end open to serve as a door. Within twenty minutes you can construct a snug hide in this manner, one that will shelter you somewhat from the elements, confine your dog if he becomes restless, and enable you to shoot comfortably in all directions. You will need to face the way the ducks flight in, and this will be determined by the wind for they always approach a pool into the wind.

Pallets make an ideal hide. (Photo: Lance Smith)

For additional comfort you can install an old chair which is far better than the usual upturned oil-drum, and perhaps construct a small shelf on which to lay out your cartridges in anticipation of some fast shooting. You need to be an optimist; a pessimist is likely to give up before this seemingly useless pool has been given a fair try.

Pool management

Just like any other shoot, your new pool will benefit from management. Vermin-control is essential. Where there are moorhens keep their numbers in check or else they will devour all the grain you tip into the shallows long before the duck show up at twilight. Constant warfare must be waged on rats who will do likewise as well as eating duck eggs and any ducklings which you are lucky enough to hatch.

Depending upon the size of your pool you might decide to rear a few duck. Duck are much more easily reared than pheasants and if brought up on a particular pool will regard it as home and flight back to feed there during the season. If you are relying on wild mallard breeding on your pool you will do well to invest in some duck-nesting baskets. These offer protection from the elements and winged vermin as well as four-footed ones if the baskets are situated, as they should be, in the water.

Feeding

If you do not feed your pool properly and regularly all your earlier work will have been for nothing. The mallard's greed is its weakness and you must exploit it. I generally begin feeding my pools about the second week in August. This is time enough to interest the duck but you will be competing against the corn harvest except in abnormal climatic conditions. A good summer means an early harvest and the sooner the stubbles are ploughed in the sooner duck will be looking to hand-fed ponds for their food. Likewise a late harvest in a wet summer will mean that you will benefit from flight-shooting until the corn is cut and the mallard turn to the stubbles. In this latter case you are likely to have a lean spell for a week or two.

Most sportsmen use barley to feed their pools. However, if you have a number of moorhen in the vicinity it is a good idea to use *whole* maize. 'Indian corn', as it is sometimes known, is too large for moorhens to swallow and thus the duck will have the benefit even if the smaller birds go to feed first.

Potatoes are a good stand-by. They need to be soft, though, and should be boiled first if hard. If you can find a farmer who wants his potato shed cleaned out before the new crop is ready, seize the opportunity eagerly. Mostly the old tubers will be soft and sprouting and can be tipped straight into the shallows. Most years I manage to obtain a supply of these potatoes. I load them into the pool and often they last for several weeks, the harder ones rotting down in the water or being rendered mushy as soon as the frosts begin. Of course, by doing this you will also encourage rats so it is best to keep a tunnel-trap or two in operation.

Any waste bread can also be used up in your pool. If you know a friendly bread shop they will probably let you have some of their stale leftovers.

The secret of feeding is to feed a little and often once the season begins in earnest. If there is corn in abundance lying in the shallows the duck will know it is there and will leave it until it is almost too dark to see before they flight, whereas a regular small amount will have the effect of bringing them in early, because they learn that the late feeders are left to glean what the early birds have not cleaned up. Feed about an hour before dusk and then retreat to a safe distance and observe how many duck come in. Your aim, once 1 September arrives, is to have a good influx of early mallard flighting in so that you can shoot a few whilst the light is still good and then leave the late-comers to feed in peace.

I seldom use duck decoys on any of my flight-ponds because if the duck know there is food in the water they will come. If their minds are made up to feed elsewhere they will go there. However, a couple of resident live decoys are ideal for drawing them, particularly a call-duck. If you cannot obtain one of these then a Khaki Campbell or two will suffice. This breed is the farmyard cousin of the mallard and will attract its wild relatives.

Always feed in the shallows. Mallard like up to a foot of water in which they can dabble and search for their food on the bottom. In deeper water the grain will lie untouched and go to waste.

Making a pool

Perhaps you have been successful in renting a small rough-shoot but to your chagrin there is no pond on it suitable for duck. All is not lost, for pools have been successfully made on dry land for a nominal cost. Indeed, once as an experiment I tried a large sheet of clear plastic, weighted down with stones and placed a few rubber decoys on it. This was done because the trees around the pond on my Forestry Commission shoot had grown tall and their shadows hid the water from the duck once the light began to fail. This artificial 'pool' was set up on a forestry road 20 yards from the water and the mallard came to it. However, for me this ploy was not one that gave me any satisfaction, merely proved a point. If you have not got a pool then make one!

The task is relatively simple on terrain that is boggy. All you need is to hire a JCB for half a day, scoop out a base, its depth depending upon the wetness below the surface, but the shallows should be no deeper than a foot at the most. You might choose to make it deeper in the middle if it is your intention to float a nesting raft or baskets.

The initial result will resemble the excavations on a building site and it may take until the following year, when the undergrowth has grown back and given it a natural look, before duck begin to use it. If possible fence it off and plant a few willows and some firs or silver-birches to provide some additional cover.

The job is not too difficult and lucky is the man who has some boggy ground on his shoot in the right place. But what of he who has firm dry ground, maybe even sloping in the very place where a flight-pond would be ideal? Such was my own problem when we moved to our present smallholding but in due course we overcame it.

The task with which I was faced was more difficult than that of most shooting men. Ours is steep, rocky terrain, the land sloping down sharply to a stream at the bottom. I toyed with the idea of blasting out part of the stream, damming it and allowing the water to trickle on down the valley at the outlet end. But this was impracticable because the boundary of our land was the centre of the stream. In the end I hired a contractor to bulldoze out about half an acre of land higher up, creating a flat shelf in the hillside and using the rubble to build up the bank on the lower side. Then the pool area was scooped out of this shelf to a depth of about a foot. Now the really difficult part was about to begin, the making of a pond which would retain rainwater for there was no other source from which to fill it.

It took me a long time locating a suitable polythene liner for this area which was approximately forty yards long by ten yards wide. In most cases the cost was prohibitive and at the back of my mind was the uneasy feeling that I was creating a white elephant, and that the outcome would be filling it all in again and re-seeding this unsightly scar on the landscape. Our initial attempt was to use a silage sheet, but the polythene was too thin and punctured, even though we had endeavoured to remove all the sharp stones beneath it. Heavy gauge polythene which builders use for damp-proofing seemed to be the answer but again we encountered a problem; we could purchase rolls of the required length but the width was a maximum of 6 yards. In the end I decided to take a chance with three rolls and overlap but I was far from happy about it.

A local haulage contractor spent a whole day ferrying sand from a nearby quarry, 32 tons in all. Sixteen tons were used as a bed for the liner, the remainder to weight it down and protect it, the polythene the sandwich in the middle. Two days' work so far and the pool itself was completed but there was much more to be done yet.

My new pool was to serve a dual purpose. As well as a flight-pond (we later decided to use it as a 'sanctuary' from which duck would disperse to use my other ponds), it would also be the home of domestic ducks and geese and

Artificially-constructed flight-pond. (Photo: Lance Smith)

house a few poultry as well. An inconspicuous shed was erected against the hedge for this latter purpose but we also had to make the pool as fox-proof as possible.

Is any fencing fox-proof except perhaps for 8 foot high steel mesh buried several inches in the ground? We substituted with strong chicken mesh, reinforced with pig-netting to give a total height of over 6 feet. I had used this same ploy with my other poultry enclosure three years earlier and had found it to be effective. I believe that the secret is in leaving the top of the fence floppy; a supporting rail would enable a marauding fox to lever itself over and back again, whereas loose wire-netting is not conducive to a marathon jump.

We began with our old farmyard goose and a pair of unpinioned mallard. The mallard stayed during the first winter, making no attempt to fly off even when the pool was frozen over, and they struck up a friendship with the goose. Spring came and the mallard left because the nesting potential was not to their liking. I then introduced a pair of Canada geese, and, with ample undergrowth inside the enclosure, I fully expected the female bird to nest; but she made no attempt because she was reluctant to venture far from the water to sit.

As the pool is filled by rainwater this works extremely well for most of the year, but in very dry weather the level does tend to drop, a combination of evaporation and some slight seepage somewhere between those overlapping

Decoy ducks and geese on the flight-pond. (Photo: Lance Smith)

polythene sheets. It was during a drought that I found the Canada's eggs, laid in the water itself.

I experimented with a nesting raft made from scrounged pallets but there was a danger of piercing the pool liner. In the meantime the odd wild mallard dropped in for a look at this new stretch of water which was very encouraging.

A flock of khaki Campbells were then introduced, primarily for the purpose of egg-laying but also to encourage these mallard to continue flighting in.

The following autumn I purchased a pair of greylags. These integrated well with the Canadas and ducks but sadly one morning one of the greys was missing. There was no sign of a fox having penetrated my fortifications so two options were left open to me; either a pinion had come off and the bird had flown away in search of freedom, or else a human predator had paid the pool a nocturnal visit. I doubt whether I shall ever know the truth.

During spells of severe weather I shut all the ducks and geese in the shed with the Rhode Island Reds. This way I can give them fresh drinking water in a trough daily and ensure their well-being. They eat surprisingly little during this incarceration because they are using little energy but overall do not seem unhappy.

A wildfowling reserve like mine is fine but the danger is in overpopulating it. The khakis have to be culled occasionally and in due course I plan to

Khaki Campbells: ideal decoys on a flight-pond. (Photo: Lance Smith)

introduce Pinkfeet geese, but if the grazing inside the enclosure becomes insufficient for the birds this will mean an increased corn bill.

I attempted to introduce some reeds from one of my other pools, but the next day there was not a single reed to be seen – the geese had grazed off the lot!

My pool has been a costly and time-consuming venture. On driving around the neighbouring countryside I see many pools, far more suited to my purpose than my own, lying neglected and overgrown. I am sure some farmers would gladly give you such a pool just to be rid of it if it was possible to move it.

Which is why there is always a good chance of securing the shooting on such a pond. Perseverance is the answer; keep looking and asking. Some day, somewhere, by the law of averages, you will be lucky.

Shooting on rivers

Rivers are the favourite haunt of wild duck, particularly in the winter time when many of the ponds and lakes are frozen. The waterways of this country are, in effect, the roadways of the wildfowl, a means of getting from one place to another. Pools are a digression, a place to go in search of food or a quiet daytime rest. If you can acquire the shooting rights along a river bank then you will surely have some sport as all rivers harbour mallard, some more than others. Duck prefer a shallow waterway with a slow current that enables them to dabble for food in comfort, and some reed-beds for cover.

You may be given permission to shoot along a river for the same reasons that we have discussed regarding flight-ponds; neither farmer nor tenant can be bothered with it. Here your scope is widened; even if duck are stubbling they will usually return to the river after feeding or follow it part of the way to their feeding ground. It is an irresistible lure but it also needs feeding in the places where you wish to attract them.

You have been granted the shooting rights on a half-mile stretch of river, so where do you start? It will be in your interests to reduce the vermin as far as possible and you may, in some areas, be troubled with feral mink. These savage creatures are a threat to all game preservation and poultry farming so you should employ gun and cage-traps against them. They are fairly easily trapped but the skins of wild mink are virtually worthless. However, you will reap your own reward by killing them.

Rivers need feeding in the same way as pools but you must choose the right place to tip your grain. You need somewhere that is shallow enough for the duck to feed and where the current will not wash the food away. I always favour a bend where the main current leaves a still backwater, perhaps some willows and reeds for cover. You may have to experiment in a number of places before you are successful.

I have had two river shoots in the past. One was fifty acres of water meadows that had previously been part of a large syndicate shoot. When they relinquished the tenancy they left their hides behind, strongly built structures with firm wooden floors and bench seats, strategically sited. But the sport did not live up to the setting and then one year the river burst its banks and flooded the meadows. That was when the duck began to come in numbers, but the Wildfowl Trust leased it and made it a sanctuary. It is now one of the most important wildfowl sanctuaries in the Midlands and I do not begrudge the Trust their acquisition for they have protected the fowl which have bred there and the sportsmen in the neighbourhood have benefited. Whereas in the beginning I only saw teal and mallard, now shoveler, tufted duck, Canada geese and wigeon use it regularly. Once a bittern was seen by a reliable ornithologist.

My other shoot was a stretch of shallow sewage river; the pollution had to be seen to be believed! On my return home my dog had to be hosed down as well as the duck I had shot. Duck were plentiful and there was an ox-bow lake at one point which they favoured. An old wartime concrete blockhouse was very conveniently situated on the edge of this, which served admirably as a hide.

You will be extremely fortunate if you manage to get permission to shoot both banks, for often rivers divide farmland. If your neighbour opposite also shoots then there is much to be gained by making his acquaintance. It will be

Four wigeon in the bag. (Photo: Calvin Williams)

to your mutual interest for you can either share the sport or else ruin it for each other. Likewise there is safety to be considered; guns on opposite banks flighting duck in the half-light can constitute a very real danger.

The bonus with river shooting is that you can shoot either morning or evening flight, or both, whereas with a pool you are restricted to evening flight. I don't advocate overshooting but once a week will not be too often. Ponds should be shot once a fortnight at the most.

If you use decoys on the river – and they can be an advantage in pulling duck in to a particular place – they need to be thrown into midstream where the shadows of the bank will not hide them, and anchored firmly. Your dog will need to be a strong swimmer and must be sent immediately a bird is down.

It was my experience that the duck always came best when the river was low. My blank days were more often than not after heavy rain when the water was high, simply because, as has already been stated, duck prefer shallow water.

Moonlight shooting

In my youth I once went on a stalk after mallard one frosty moonlight night. My imagination was fired by reading of Bill Powell's moonlit experiences on the Solway shores and the nearest I could manage to that was my small flight-pond.

It was a thrilling experience to be abroad after midnight in a silent silvery world. I moved cautiously, my footsteps sounding as though I was walking on crispy breakfast cereal, my dog at heel. My pulses raced when I heard the guttural sounds of feeding mallard and the last 50 yards to the edge of the reeds took me something like twenty minutes.

I risked a peep; there they were, a dozen or more duck feeding in the one patch of water that was still open where the spring fed the pool. The dog moved, the mallard jumped and I let off a double shot. Remus retrieved one bird, went back again and found a second fluttering in the reeds.

I was euphoric. My plan had worked, I would try it again the next full moon. The only trouble was that when the next full moon arrived there were no duck using my pool. I had not seen one since that night and it was weeks before I saw another. Night-shooting had cost me dearly.

My theory is that all the duck that were feeding on the pool over the weeks were there that night, the 'local population', in fact, and the survivors had a scare that they remembered for some time to come. Since then I have never attempted to shoot a flight-pond in the moonlight.

If, however, the full moon rises around dusk it is always worthwhile stopping on an extra half hour to see if duck are flighting. You might be lucky; on the other hand they have several hours of bright moonlight ahead of them so there is no hurry.

Ideally one needs a background of white fleecy cloud to be able to see duck on the wing. On cloudless nights you will only spot them if they cross the face of the moon. Conditions have to be right. The foreshore is the best place, followed by the river. But leave the ponds in peace.

Shooting on lakes

A lake is in effect a gigantic flight-pond. Perhaps duck will sometimes use it for a day-roost if it is large enough and they can sit out in the middle unmolested. But basically the inland fowler is restricted to evening flights and these will be far more tricky than the small pool where the duck will be in range from whichever direction they come.

Wind direction is a vital factor. In stormy weather the birds like somewhere sheltered from the wind and that small bay below the pine woods could be just the place. Feed it in readiness for the next gale and try your luck.

If the lake is big enough then it may well stand the odd morning flight. The criteria is not to disturb duck that are using it. Watch carefully and see where they are flighting off and the odd shot or two on a windy morning won't be detrimental. On some of the larger syndicate shoots where duck are hand-reared the day's sport usually begins with a duck shoot, the guns lining one end of the big pool whilst the beaters put the birds on the wing. The sport is brief; it cannot be otherwise. Wild duck are more wary than the reared ones and will take to the wing at the first sign of danger, heading for quieter places. The reared duck will, as likely as not, circle round and drop back on the water. That is the difference between wildfowling and duck-shooting.

Where to find shooting on lakes

A useful initial move is to approach water authorities who own large reservoirs. Usually the fishing is let on these for high prices but the shooting may have been overlooked. You may be lucky enough to obtain permission to shoot during the winter months when there will not be many fishermen present. At least it is worth a try.

Another source is the gravel pit, a result of the quarrying that has disfigured the rural scene. At least perhaps one can glean something from it! Often these excavations fill with water, are left, and the undergrowth grows back. Many of them are deep, dangerous, and of no use whatsoever to the shooting man. But some have a shallow end which duck can dabble in. I know of some of these marl-holes which are frequented by Canada geese. It is worthwhile exploring the possibility and if you know of something that looks suitable contact the owners.

INLAND DUCK SHOOTING

Daytime duck-shooting

Some years ago during the early part of the season I motored down to spend a day on my shoot. My first task was to go and feed the small flight-pond in the forest. On my approach six mallard jumped and I took a right and left. I had a walk round the woods, paused for lunch, and later in the afternoon I chanced to pass the pool again. Four mallard rose and I dropped another couple.

Towards evening I returned to the pool to await the evening flight and much to my amazement I surprised another couple of duck, both of which ended up in the bag! Had I shot the original six which were determined to return to that pond in spite of being shot at? Or were duck just dropping in throughout the day? I do not know but the fact is that I shot six duck between flighting times.

Nowadays dusk is an awkward time for me to shoot due to smallholding duties, when there are poultry to be shut up and goats to be milked, so most of my duck are shot during the day.

Mallard like somewhere quiet to rest up during the daylight hours. Often they use a river or a large lake but if they know of a remote pool where there is an abundant supply of food they will, from time to time, use that also.

I believe that duck shot during the day create far less disturbance to pools than dusk flighting, simply because only the odd birds are to be found there; you do not scare off those that flight in at twilight.

Stubbling duck

For a few weeks of the year duck desert their routine of feeding on pools to gorge themselves on the stubble fields where there is an ample supply of corn for the taking. If you can find such a field (and you will only do it by persistent reconnaissance in the later part of the day with binoculars) you might just obtain permission to have a go at them. A farmer may be more agreeable to giving permission for the odd night's shooting rather than for a whole season. And if you were lucky enough to make a bag then he might extend his welcome even further when you call and offer him some birds.

The procedure is very much like pigeon-shooting. You need a good hide, some decoys if you are to bring the duck in range of your gun and you will need a good dog to pick up your birds. A wounded duck will head for the nearest water even if it is only a drainage ditch that runs alongside the field.

Wild duck offer an immense choice of shooting inland. They are unpredictable and the magical sound of those fast wingbeats will have your pulses racing. Mallard are a valuable source of food, lean meat as opposed to their fatty farmyard cousins. Truly a bird of the wild, they belong to nobody, and if you can find somewhere to shoot them then you are entitled to some.

121

CHAPTER NINE

The Smallholding Shoot

All too often the sporting potential of smallholdings is dismissed by the shooting man. An acreage of anything from five to fifty is considered too small to offer anything in the way of shooting. Nothing could be further from the truth; it is the quality of the 'pocket-handkerchief' shoot that counts, its location, its layout. Gamebirds recognise no boundaries, if a field is attractive to them it matters not whether it forms part of a large estate or is merely an adjacent privately-owned patch of rough.

When considering the prospect of finding some shooting on a smallholding, there is one factor very much in your favour; the smallholder is unlikely to have let his shooting for the reasons already stated and he is probably far too busy to spend much time with a gun himself except in an attempt to kill vermin, and he might just be very glad to find somebody who is willing to do that for him!

My own shoot consists of our own seven and a half acre holding, plus some rented adjoining land comprising a Forestry Commission wood and twenty-seven acres of boggy inland marsh, all at a height of 1,200 feet above sea level. But for the purpose of this chapter we will merely concentrate on the smallholding itself, which, for much of the time, is all I have time to shoot anyway.

My land is steeply sloping with a valley and a small stream the lower boundary. One side adjoins thick Forestry Commission woods of which I rent the shooting, the other a tall roadside hedge. The land is divided up between old pastureland with seeding grass that is grazed by goats and a donkey, a recently planted spinney of silver-birch with conifers for a wind-break, a patch of arable where we grow organic vegetables on raised beds, and the poultry and duck-pool section. Overall it is an interesting mixture, considering that some eight years ago it was all just pasture grazed by sheep.

Ours is an island in the midst of commercial sheep and mixed farming, surrounded by desecrated hedgerows (if they have not already been bulldozed out to make larger fields to create an even greater mountain of surplus grain), fields that have been sprayed until there are precious few minerals left in

The smallholding shoot. (Photo: Lance Smith)

The smallholding shoot offers a wide variety of cover to attract game.
(Photo: Lance Smith)

them, and an absence of plant and insect life. Ours is basically a non-meat producing holding which is run as a shoot also. In effect it is a kind of 'compromise' shoot.

We ourselves do not eat domestically reared meat apart from free-range poultry and game, not out of any emotive reasons but because we consider that there is too high a level of cholesterol and harmful additives in farm meat today. Combining all this with 100 per cent organically-grown crops means that most of our customers are vegetarians. It always seems to me that in the sporting press vegetarians are automatically associated with animal rights demonstrators and agitators whilst in fact nothing could be further from the truth. Indeed, my wife was a vegetarian before we were married and she never objected to shooting. Nowadays she is the holder of a shotgun certificate. Our customers are fully aware that we shoot and we have never once had an objection raised on this issue. I was interested to read an article by a noteworthy doctor in a leading health magazine some years ago to the effect that he shot regularly to provide wild meat, which is low in cholesterol, for his family for exactly the same reasons that I do.

Planning a small shoot

Our smallholding shoot is carefully planned, even to the extent of putting down a few birds each year for we work on the principle that we have to sow before we can reap. A couple of years ago we began substituting pheasants with guineafowl but this is something of a more detailed experiment which we shall deal with in the next chapter.

Nevertheless, the shooting has to be planned carefully for on a small acreage haphazard shooting would result in very little in the bag. And the land in question has to be made to serve a worthwhile shooting foray, or otherwise a half-hour walk would cover the ground with nothing to show for it.

Go for the pool first. If there are any duck on it they will soon be up and away at the first shot. In my case we check the common pool by the roadside for our own is a small sanctuary. After that we walk the banks of the stream at the bottom. There is not enough water for duck but it holds a pheasant or two and there are always woodcock there after the November moon. A shot at pigeon is almost always guaranteed and if necessary we can come back later and loft a few decoys on the edge of the big forest.

Now it is time to tackle the steep slope. There are partridge here most days, and usually the covey runs forward to a couple of tall spreading oaks and chooses the exact moment to spring when your field of vision is obscured. To combat that we leave a gun on the lower side and he will get a shot at genuine driven partridge! The birds cross the valley, alight on the fields opposite, but you can bet the brace in the bag that they will be back tomorrow. They return because they are not harassed; I am aware that they are on my land most of the time but I only try for a shot at them occasionally.

I planted the spinney for the convenience of shooting. Long and narrow, any pheasants in it will strike out in the direction of the big forest so we leave a gun on that side. We take our time beating it through, add a cock pheasant to the bag and a couple of hens get away in the direction anticipated. That is fine; like the partridge, they will be back.

Now it is time to go and try for a rabbit in the thick gorse. There is a fair-sized patch of gorse and we must allow the dog ample time to work it. The rabbits, if any, will bolt uphill; only on the very odd occasion have I known one go downhill towards the stream.

After that we try the crops. The biggest bonus of all in my opinion is a patch of Jerusalem artichokes. I have even planted them in the spinney as they are an irresistible draw for pheasants, offering both dense cover and food. The plants grow to a height of 6 feet, the tops dying off with the approach of winter. Pheasants love to scratch down to the knobbly potato-like tubers and peck at them.

Tubers will cost about 10p each from a garden shop but are a good investment because if left in the ground they spread rapidly, and the following year you will have three times your first crop. They are good eating too, with possibly an acquired taste, having a smoky-earthy flavour. We use them for soup, eat them baked, or roast them along with duck, pheasant or guineafowl.

The afternoon has been a casual one and now we can finish up with a duck-flight on that roadside pool. It is fed regularly, shot sparingly, and having watched mallard dropping in to feed on the previous evening I am hopeful of providing a shot or two for my companion(s).

Thus we have had quite a memorable day on this 'pocket-handkerchief' shoot, all the more satisfying because each shot has been savoured. We have made the most of every square yard of ground and perhaps next time we shall have a go at the pigeons. But today there has been no time!

Over the years my attitude towards shooting has changed. In the days before we lived here and I used to make a 140-mile round-trip for my shooting, the emphasis was more on the size of the bag, which was only natural taking into account travelling time and expense, plus the fact that I had to cram my sport into one day a week. Nowadays, though, I only shoot to fulfil our needs which are modest.

I cannot remember when I last shot for a whole day. Usually it is an hour or two hours three times a week, and I am more than happy with a brace of birds for Sunday lunch or the freezer. Often with a brace in the bag I call it a day for I like to see pheasants about the place. A hard day's shooting could easily put paid to the prospects for the rest of the season and I would far sooner spread my enjoyment out over the winter months.

125

Although I regard shooting as part and parcel of smallholding, I would not consider it as a commercial enterprise. Certainly surplus rabbits will be sold because I am compelled to control them but I do not wish the sporting side of my lifestyle to become a monetary issue. We farm organically on principle; likewise we conserve for the same reason.

Field sports, farming and conservation are a blend which make up the rural scene. The removal of any one of these would upset the entire balance and jeopardise the future of our wildlife, something which those so vigorously opposed to country sports either cannot or will not see. Although these campaigners are in a minority, their tiny voice is dangerous, a whisper that could influence the non-sporting yet reasonable faction. I cannot understand why these protestors do not direct their efforts at the chemicals which are so detrimental to wildlife in general. *Insecticides and herbicides kill far more birds and animals than ever the shooting community will.*

It is all a question of respecting each other's rights, attempting to understand the point of view of others and not being dogmatic. With the right approach we can all live in harmony and relegate the anti-everything brigade to faint whispers in the wilderness.

Finding a smallholding shoot

There are innumerable smallholdings throughout the length and breadth of Great Britain. Again it will be necessary to go out in the car and make a systematic search.

Look for roadside produce signs; eggs, goats' milk, vegetables, etc. You have a ready-made excuse here to contact the smallholder; call and buy a dozen eggs or a pint of milk. Most of these small farmers in rural areas are pleased to see callers, not simply for the sale but because they like to talk to somebody. You can tactfully steer the conversation round to shooting and see what the prospects are.

Now that you are hunting smaller acreages, you can generally see from the house what the land has to offer. Preferably ignore market-garden smallholdings for the reasons stated earlier. Look for a small area of woodland, perhaps that pool which nobody seems to want. Root crops will hold gamebirds and if there is a river passing through you can be sure that duck will use it at some time.

Don't be in a rush. Country folk are suspicious of anybody who appears to be in a hurry. If you ascertain that nobody actually shoots the land it might be good policy to refrain from mentioning your direct interest and return the following week for some more produce. If you become a regular customer at the farm gate you are half way to obtaining some shooting.

If you are offered just pigeon and vermin shooting to begin with, don't look a gift-horse in the mouth. Respect the game, especially where a smallholding borders an estate or shoot leased to a syndicate which rears pheasants. Even if you have permission to kill game, shooting those that stray from a neighbouring shoot will almost certainly have repercussions. In all probability, once the syndicate realise what is happening, they will step in with a higher offer for the shooting of your smallholding to put a stop to it.

Another point to bear in mind is that the smallholder is not a wealthy farmer with large subsidy cheques arriving with regularity. In many cases he has to take a job and leave his wife to look after the holding. Money is not plentiful and if he can let his shooting he will probably be delighted.

Ascertain that the farmer is authorised to lease the sporting rights. Some smallholders are tenants and often the land is owned by a county council. If you are shooting without the landlord's permission, you could find yourself in trouble. Ultimately the tenant is responsible for his actions in letting you shoot, but there is bound to be some unpleasantness.

Intensive shooting

This is intensive shooting which must not be confused with over-shooting. You must adopt a systematic approach as I have outlined already. You must shoot sparingly with the exception of pigeon and vermin. Every foray must be planned if your sport is to last the season.

I am apt to regard my smallholding shoot as separate from my adjoining leased land which is one of the reasons why I decided to introduce guineafowl as a game bird, and this will be described in the following chapter.

127

CHAPTER TEN

Guineafowl Shooting

Guineafowl are both a fascinating and comical bird, the common variety being pearl grey, unmistakable by their jerky head movements and call that sounds like '*get-back, get-back, get-back*'. They belong to the *Galliformes* species which includes grouse, pheasant, turkey and the farmyard chicken. They have the traits of the latter birds, a strange mixture of congregating in flocks, strong fliers and can be either tame or wild according to their habitat. You can keep them as poultry or rear them as sporting birds, such is their adaptability. Above all, they are excellent watchdogs and will raise the alarm deafeningly at the approach of a human intruder or a predator.

Our first batch of guineafowl were acquired by swapping a goatling for six adult birds. The man who bought the young goat from us had only one shed and the occupants of this were six guineas, so we had the birds in exchange. They ran with the poultry in the field for almost a year before they decided that they preferred a wilder existence in the forest nearby. So they deserted the sheds for the tall pines.

Pheasants are difficult to hold on high ground such as ours and on more than one occasion with the onset of hard weather our hand-reared birds have wandered down to the valleys in spite of regular feeding. So I decided to give guineafowl a try, semi-domesticated ones that would serve both for the pot and some regular shooting.

I hatched a few under Silkies and bought in some poults to supplement them. They are incredibly easy to rear and much hardier than pheasants. At a few days old they were running free-range with the mother hens and virtually fending for themselves. They were thrown a few handfuls of chick crumbs for the first week but after that they gleaned for themselves and grew rapidly.

The species originated from Africa but they are at home in virtually every country of the world, even the coldest of climates. They like to roost in tall trees, choosing the same ones even after the leaf has fallen. I have seen them during the winter, living balls of snow that awake at dawn, shake themselves and drop down to feed.

Guineafowl are under-rated as sporting birds. (Photo: Lance Smith)

Guineafowl are superb eating. (Photo: Lance Smith)

129

Once you have an established flock you should have little need to hatch the eggs under broodies. The hens will wander off and lay in a clump of thick nettles somewhere and the next time you see them will be when they emerge with a batch of chicks. In theory! The atrocious summer of 1985 was a marked exception; our birds, which had already been reduced to a basic stock by shooting, showed no inclination to rear broods. Instead they laid eggs just about anywhere and the majority of those were infertile. So we ended up buying-in poults again.

Unlike pheasants, guineafowl will almost always return home from their daily foraging. We lost the odd ones to vermin, mostly young poults that fell prey to buzzards, but overall they survived well. They can be a nuisance in a field of corn, seeming to have a systematic method of 'harvesting' a patch for themselves. I have watched them about it, jumping at the stalks, pulling them down and eating the ears of grain. They glean for themselves and all you need is a few handfuls of corn daily to remind them where their home is.

Shooting

The first time I saw a guineafowl shot was on a driven shoot to which I had been invited. A flock of them came out high and fast ahead of the pheasants and one of the guns knocked one down. It cost him a fiver, for there was a fine for anybody who shot a guinea, but he did not seem to mind. In all probability he had been asked by his wife to bring one home for the Sunday lunch table.

I was impressed by the way the birds flew, the sporting shots which they presented, and I was already thinking of how they could be shown on the steep terrain back home. The only problem sometimes is getting them to take to the wing but they share that reluctance with pheasants. It is soon remedied; a good dog will get them to fly and all you need to do is to drive them from steep land across a small valley and you have unrivalled high birds.

Here Muffin, my Springer spaniel, proved her worth. I have purposely allowed her to range wide on steep hillsides whilst I walk along the bottom and all that is necessary is to make sure that the guineafowl are fed on the top slope. Once they are there is it a relatively simple matter to send the dog up to them and I can enjoy driven shooting all on my own! I rarely shoot more than a brace, usually on Saturday morning so that they can be plucked and dressed in time for lunch the next day. However, I did experience some problems a few days prior to one Christmas.

We had decided to give dressed guineafowl as Christmas presents to some of our friends. Indeed, the birds were promised and on the eve of the day when I was due to shoot them a disconcerting thought struck me. Bagging a brace for lunch was no problem but to shoot seven or eight presented

Driven from the upper slopes guineafowl offer some high shots.
(Photo: Lance Smith)

difficulties because once shot at the flock disperses, usually on to my neighbour's land, and the next time they are seen is when they are back roosting in the trees.

I had to get some birds and there was only one answer. They would have to be 'poached' on our own smallholding. So, after dark that night I went out with the air-rifle, accompanied by one of my sons whose job was to shine the torch. Unsporting as it seemed, I was interested to see how I would fare 'Kenzie-style'. My late wildfowling guide had often related how he had gone to the coverts of some East Anglian estate and filled a sack with pheasants on a dark, windy night in no time at all.

The guineas were perched on the branches about fifteen feet up, and my son directed the torch beam on to one. I took aim, there was a scarcely audible 'ping' and the bird thudded down. I did not even have time to congratulate myself before the whole roosting flock burst into the air with a deafening clamour and flew blindly in all directions. Where the majority went I had no idea, only that a few, enough for my needs, landed on our roof and that of our neighbour's hay barn, scrabbling their way up the slates until they found a perch.

They were too high for the .177 now, so we went indoors and fetched the .410. I envisaged another flurry of wings as I cracked the first one down but they never moved this time. I followed the torchlight, shooting and reloading until we had enough for our needs, much to my relief. But I am still intrigued as to why they scattered for the near-silent pellet gun yet never moved when I used the small shotgun. It was an interesting, if rather unsporting, experiment very necessary for the season of goodwill.

Advantages of guineafowl over pheasants

Apart from their eagerness to return home to roost at the end of the day, guineafowl have other advantages over the pheasant. I would say without any reservations that I consider the guineafowl to be superior eating to the pheasant as well as being up to a pound heavier when dressed. That delicate gamey flavour incorporates the taste of cockerel, gamebird and chicken. If you want to rear and shoot them on a semi-commercial basis there is a ready market for them; many of the better restaurants today feature them on the menu.

Guineafowl attract game. On more than one occasion I have noticed both partridges and pheasants gleaning amongst my flock on the stubble field opposite my house. In fact, this last season we saw more game in the vicinity than ever before, in December and January when usually the pheasants have deserted us for the warmer climate of lower ground.

Of course, guineafowl make an awful lot of noise and never seem to stop calling even when feeding, and in more populated areas than ours there might be complaints from residents who do not appreciate the presence of these birds. Often passing tourists park their cars to sit and watch my birds, or are forced to halt because they are gritting on the road, and these people frequently remark, 'What lovely birds! What *are* they?' Yet I guarantee that if these strangers had a flock close to their home the owner's telephone would rarely stop ringing as the complaints poured in. One local cottager did remark to me that my guineafowl were all perching on her roof and that she had to throw stones up at them to move them. But, after all, that is all part of country life!

I doubt whether guineafowl will ever replace the pheasant as a sporting bird except on smallholding shoots such as my own. But shooting with land above 800 feet one would do worse than to consider the prospect. Guineafowl will not wander far and if you are running a small shoot on a restricted budget they are certainly value for money.

Introducing guineafowl to your shoot

If you have managed to rent the shooting of a small farm, particularly a smallholding, you must discuss the prospect of rearing guineafowl with the farmer. He may or may not be enthusiastic about the project simply because there is every chance that the guineas will desert their intended spinney home and return to the farm buildings. They can become a noisy nuisance but, more important, they will run with the poultry and soon increase his corn bill!

Unless you have regular access to the farm you need to rear your guineafowl in a run on the lawn at home. For the first few weeks they will not make sufficient noise to become a nuisance to neighbours in a suburban area.

All you need is a coop and run and a good broody hen. I would again advocate the use of a Silky. The incubation period is roughly twenty-five days but the eggs may hatch over a period of forty-eight hours so be patient and leave the mother hen to her own business. The less you disturb her, the better.

I prefer not to wash eggs collected for hatching as the embryo may become damaged. A Silky will sit about eight eggs comfortably, depending upon her size. Do not be tempted to put more under her as some will become chilled and it will not always be the same eggs as she turns them; the majority of the clutch could become chilled in rotation.

You will need chick crumbs for the first three weeks if your *keets* (guineafowl chicks/poults) are confined to a run. Treat them very much as you would pheasants and aim to move them to your shoot at about six weeks. They will need a release-pen of some kind and it is a good idea to put the mother hen in a coop with them for a further fortnight.

The keets will learn to go up to roost much easier than pheasants will. You can also run guineas in with pheasants as many gamekeepers do. The advantages are many; they will teach the pheasant poults to go up to roost and the latter will be less inclined to stray if they run with the flock.

There is a myth that guineafowl will deter foxes with their alarm cry of 'get-back, get-back'. I do not believe this as I have lost guineafowl to foxes. But they will certainly utter a warning when a fox or other predator is in the immediate vicinity and the pheasants will learn to recognise this alarm call.

The diet of the guineafowl is varied. If there is a ready supply of corn the birds will not go far away. They will hunt insects all day long and are attracted to green crops. We have to net our raised-beds which grow such crops; they will eat swede tops right down to the swede but will ignore parsnips. However their constant scratching in the garden is a nuisance and one year we had an excessive number of green potatoes where they had dislodged the mounds.

Greenstuff is essential to their well-being and if they are kept in confinement they should be given a few cabbage leaves or seeded lettuce daily. Most greengrocers will be only to happy to supply you with these. I have an arrangement whereby I collect such waste every day, mostly for the turkeys.

A good release-pen and ample feeding might just ensure that your guineafowl remain in the wood or spinney and do no more than pay the farmyard an occasional visit.

Of course if you can persuade the farmer that guineafowl could be to your mutual advantage then you are on to a winner. Work out some kind of 'partnership'; you rear the birds and he feeds them. Your reward will be in the sport that they offer and you might be able to come to some arrangement whereby you go half-shares on the proceeds of the sale of birds to an hotel or restaurant. That would be an ideal set-up because you may well find that you get your shooting for nothing, or very little, as a result and you can always include a few pheasants in your programme as variety.

Of course the rearing of guineafowl on a commercial basis is an entirely different proposition which I do not intend to go into in this book for it would be of very little interest to the sportsman. But a flock of free-ranging guineas which provide both sport and a small income would be handy for both farmer and shooting tenant.

Even if the idea of rearing guineafowl as the nucleus of sport on a small shoot does not appeal to you, it will be to your advantage to have one or two running with your pheasants. They will help to keep your birds at home as well as acting as a lookout for danger. Also, their movements may well determine the whereabouts of your pheasants.

CHAPTER ELEVEN

Poachers!

Every shooting man must be conversant with the basic laws relating to poaching and be aware of the threat which these criminals present to the rural scene. Gone are the days of the romantic Robin Hood-type poacher, the 'moocher', whose only concern was to snare a rabbit or shoot a pheasant for his own dinner. He has been replaced by ruthless gangs who will not stop at violence, even murder, in a racket where the rewards are lucrative.

If you rent a shoot, whether it be just a small rough-shoot or a larger syndicate shoot, then the odds are that at some time you will be troubled with poaching on some scale. You must be prepared and it is necessary to have some plan of action in mind before the occasion arises.

Prior to the Armed Trespass Bill poaching was considered to be a minor offence. The poacher needed to be caught with game or rabbits on him for the police to take any positive action, otherwise a charge of 'trespassing in pursuit of conies' was the usual charge brought which often resulted in a derisory fine. One stood a better chance of a prosecution if the offender was apprehended with game on his person when the Game Laws could be used; perhaps a pheasant had been shot without a game licence, maybe even on a Sunday. Even if the police were in a position to 'throw the book' at the poacher the fines were negligible, except in the case of night-poaching which even in those days carried the possibility of a prison sentence.

But the Armed Trespass Bill gave the police the power to enter on private land to apprehend anyone carrying a gun there without permission. The poacher does not even need to have fired a shot; he can be arrested and taken to a police station, and charged. Even now, though, magistrates in a few cases do not treat poaching as seriously as they should, but at long last in some instances the penalties are severe. Fines can run into several hundred pounds and where violence is used the criminal (for such he is) sometimes receives a prison sentence.

Stiffer penalties have served to make the poacher more desperate. If he can resist capture, he will. Gone are the days when the sportsman who came upon poachers during the course of a day's shooting could demand names and addresses without undue risk to himself. Poachers must be apprehended and brought before a court wherever possible but all the pheasants on your shoot are not worth personal injury, or worse. So some degree of caution is necessary.

Whenever possible contact the police and bring them to the scene as quickly as possible, and do not approach the poachers yourself. This is not easy in remote rural areas and often by the time the law shows up the poachers have got away; even if they are traced it will be very difficult to prove a case that will stand up in court.

The most important thing is to take a vehicle registration number. Most poachers use a vehicle unless they are a local gang. If you hear shots, before going to investigate check on the points of access to your shoot and look for a car or van parked on a roadside verge. You get a 'nose' for recognising poachers' vehicles; it is unlikely, unless they are complete amateurs, that gun cases, cartridge boxes, etc., will be on view. Look for a general untidiness,

The folding .410 shotgun is easily concealed by the poacher. (Photo: Lance Smith)

sacks, boots, evidence of a dog. Always carry a pencil and notebook and record the registration number, make and colour of vehicle. Then without further loss of time find a telephone.

It is always handy to have the police on the scene anyway. There is always the chance that you might actually *know* the poachers. Suppose it was a neighbouring farmer or one of his labourers; there might be considerable embarrassment on both parts if you caught him and as a result you might agree to let him off with a warning. In which case he would probably take more care not to be caught next time. You would merely have served to make him more wary and the poaching would continue. But once the police are called the matter is out of your hands. They will usually prosecute unless there is a lack of evidence and unless the culprit pleads guilty you will be called as a witness. The whole business is conducted properly right from the start and you will be spared arguments and excuses. All the same, prevention is better than cure.

Preventing poaching

In days gone by one of the gamekeeper's duties was night-watching. This entailed spending long hours out in the coverts on a winter's night, usually during the weeks prior to Christmas. It was a cold, tiring business and there was little chance to catch up on lost sleep during the daytime for the routine duties would not wait. Many keepers still patrol after dark but there are sophisticated devices on the market today which can eliminate a lot of this.

Poacher alarms can be purchased at varying costs, depending upon how much land you have to cover. Mostly it is just the main coverts which are protected by these, ringed by an invisible circuit which triggers off a warning in the keeper's cottage if there is an intruder on the preserves. The system also pinpoints the poacher's exact whereabouts and this means that explicit directions can be passed on to the police.

Alarm-guns have been on the market for many years, a trip-wire attached to a gun which detonates a blank cartridge. Usually this will serve to scare off the nocturnal intruder; the professional poacher learns how to spot an alarm gun, knows the places where one is likely to be set. If he sets one off then usually he has ample time to make his getaway.

It is most unlikely that the poachers will use shotguns; their weapons will be .22 rifles fitted with sound-moderators and they will choose a stormy night. Romantic as moonlight poaching may sound, roosting pheasants are far more likely to be disturbed and fly. It is virtually impossible to walk through any wood in the dark without making a noise of some kind. Only a strong wind will deaden the sounds made by a night-time marauder. If he does not have moonlight then he must use a torch at some time and so if you are patrolling watch out for a light being shone.

.22 rifle fitted with a silencer: ideal for shooting roosting pheasants at night.
(Photo: Lance Smith)

But better still to concentrate on adjacent roads, gateways and lay-bys. There is sure to be a vehicle around somewhere.

Lampers

My first experience with lampers came about one November morning at about 3 am. I was awakened by the bedroom being lit up as though a parked car was outside in the road with its headlights elevated at the window. On getting up to investigate I saw that two powerful lamps were sweeping across the grazing fields opposite. Although I did not rent the shooting of this land I was fully aware that whoever was out there was poaching, and in all probability they would work across my own land. My first phone call was to the farmer. He was not interested in shooting so I told him that I thought that somebody was rustling his sheep (poachers are often common thieves as well), and this was sure to bring him hotfoot from the farmhouse almost two miles away. Next I phoned the police; the local officer was off duty so my call had to be switched to the main police station eighteen miles away. Therefore I could hardly expect to see the law in less than half an hour.

With hindsight I might have pulled the Land Rover across the road and created an obstruction. I didn't and ten minutes later, just before the farmer arrived, a Mini van, being driven on sidelights only, crept past our house. The birds had flown; we were too late.

Although any form of night-poaching is serious, I am inclined to regard this episode as amateurish. We do not have deer on Black Hill and gangs which infest the Ludlow area would surely have known this. I believe that they were after rabbits, perhaps even a reconnaissance foray to ascertain if there were coneys in sufficient numbers up here to warrant poaching. The rabbits have never recovered from a serious outbreak of myxomatosis eight years ago and we have very few hares; consequently I was not surprised that the lampers never troubled us again.

Lampers usually work with lurchers and a man who knows his business and has a good dog can make a considerable bag in a night. There are no shots to arouse a sleeping neighbourhood but the lamps are a sure giveaway – if anybody is awake to notice them! The poachers usually wait until the very early hours of the morning before commencing operations. All the same, I find it hard to believe that nobody sees the lights. The public are strangely apathetic, look for an obvious solution or don't even bother at all. They see lights sweeping the fields – perhaps it is the farmer checking his stock but it's none of their business so they let it pass. It could well be their business for these nocturnal villains are likely to steal anything they come across and it is in *everybody's* interests to get this form of poaching stamped out.

Of course, there are legitimate lampers who obtain permission to hunt land and are worthy fieldsportsmen. I am sure that these latter would not object to being checked out occasionally if it meant that poaching gangs were apprehended as a result.

Shooting from vehicles

The small shoot owner is most likely to be pestered by motorised poaching, particularly early on Sunday mornings. This is the work of amateurs, often frustrated shooters who have not bothered to look for legitimate shooting and whom the sport would be better off without anyway. There can be neither monetary reward nor satisfaction in these operations.

Usually the offenders choose a fairly remote rural area; one drives slowly along the lanes, his companion in the passenger seat with a loaded shotgun between his knees, maybe even poking out of the window. There might even be poachers on the back seat also, primed to shoot.

They spy a cock pheasant feeding in a field. The driver stops, the bird is blasted, one of them dashes to retrieve it and they drive off at full speed. Nothing clever in that, and it is certainly not worth the risk of being caught for the proverbial book will be thrown at the offenders; armed trespass, shooting from a highway, no game licence, shooting game on the sabbath, and the fines will be in the region of one or two hundred pounds. And if the magistrates really understand the game preserves they may well order guns and vehicle to be confiscated as well. All for a pheasant which did not even offer a sporting shot!

The only sure way to combat this type of poaching is by forsaking that Sunday morning lie-in and being vigilant. If you have seen pheasant feathers close to the road it is a sure bet that you are being poached in this way. Take a companion with you because a witness will come in handy; hide both your vehicle and yourselves and watch and wait. All you need is the poachers' registration number and the sooner you report it, the better. A CB radio can come in very handy, both for keeping in contact with your colleague, so that you can cover a wider area, and for raising the alarm.

Deer poaching

Although this book is not about deer is it only fair to warn any shooting tenant about the dangers of deer poaching because if there are deer in the vicinity you could well come up against these dangerous villains and they are not to be treated lightly.

Deer present a profitable income to the poacher. A carcass can fetch upwards of £100 on the black market and a gang who sleep during the daylight hours and poach at night can make a lot of money. One cause for concern is the amount of suffering inflicted upon the deer. Snares may be set which will catch an animal by the leg and it will be in agony for hours, even days if the gang become suspicious of police or forest rangers patrolling an area, when the criminals will desert and leave their wires set.

Or they will shoot from vehicles at night. They will not bother to follow up a wounded deer in the manner which a legitimate stalker will; they will drive on and look for the next one to show itself. But these are the casuals, men who consider a carcass a good night's work. The professionals will use dogs and lamps and will kill (and wound) an awful lot more deer. It will be no hit-and-miss affair; the herds will have been watched, confederates will be employed as decoys to draw the police away from the scene of the intended crime. And if the poachers are cornered they will not give up without a fight.

Make a habit of taking the numbers of all parked vehicles. Treat it as a 'hobby' just as perhaps you once collected train numbers. Numbers which crop up repeatedly should be investigated by the police and they will welcome anybody who keeps a watchful eye and informs them of anything suspicious.

It is in your own interests to be vigilant where poaching is concerned, even away from your own shoot. Or if you don't have a shoot at all. Who knows, it could well earn you an invitation to shoot with a grateful tenant or landowner . . .

CHAPTER TWELVE

Foxes

The only surviving member of the wolf family in Great Britain is the red fox. We are all familiar with this handsome creature if only on Christmas cards against a snowy background. Reynard has been given a kind of Robin Hood role in the countryside even if he only plunders to feed himself and his family. He has been associated with cunning and bravery and enjoys a status which endears him to townspeople. The anti-fieldsports brigade would have the fox protected, as would many other misinformed people in suburbia who don't have to worry about losing poultry, game or newly-born lambs to this ruthless predator.

I once read a claim somewhere that foxes and pheasants could live side-by-side. Maybe they could if there was a 10-foot steel-mesh fence separating them, the bottom buried in the ground! Foxes are a drain on the rural economy. It costs money to keep them at bay and when you are woken in the middle of the night by a dog-fox barking or a vixen howling, you toss restlessly in your bed and wonder if your pheasants are safe on their roosts or if your poultry-shed is secure. The sheep farmer worries about newly-born lambs for the fox will plunder mercilessly; he is kill-crazy, kills for the sake of it. If he finds a way into the poultry shed he won't be content with taking the odd bird for food; he will slaughter the lot, leave you to find a mass of feathered headless bodies the next morning.

I am always pleased to see an abundance of rabbits because when there is food in plenty in the wild, foxes will often be content to take their natural prey and the poultry farmer can sleep easier in his bed. But a landowner can be fined for harbouring rabbits, or his neighbour may make a claim against him for damage to growing crops. The man from the Ministry will arrive post-haste with his tin of cymag gas and gas the warrens. But the man who harbours foxes on his land is allowed to do so with impunity, no matter that they ravage the adjacent poultry farm or take young lambs.

If you have a shoot then you must control your foxes and in some areas this is a controversial matter. The local hunt like to see a fox during their winter meets and can do a useful job, but the fact is there are foxes for everybody

Free-range geese: easy prey for foxes. (Photo: Lance Smith)

and no matter how many you kill there will always be some left for the hunting fraternity.

Where you have free-range poultry you cannot afford to have foxes. Once Reynard is aware of your birds he will not let up in his endeavours to kill them. My own experience is that he is persistent rather than cunning although extremely wary.

Snaring

Snaring is probably the most effective way of reducing foxes. I stress at the outset that I do not like snaring but it is very necessary. Remember, *the self-locking snare is now illegal* and you can only use the free-running variety.

There are codes of practice relating to snaring which must be observed. Your wires must be inspected twice a day, morning and evening preferably, because if somebody comes upon a fox pulling and struggling in a wire they will doubtless report you. Also, your aim is to cause a minimum of suffering; you want the fox dead.

Never set snares close to a road, footpath or public right of way. If you do then invariably somebody's dog will get caught. This happened recently in our area; a fox-snare with a heavy-duty chain had been set in a roadside hedgerow, and an elderly widow was out walking her ageing dog when the

Setting a fox-snare in a hedge on a well-used run. (Photo: Lance Smith)

animal got caught. Fortunately, help was at hand and the dog suffered no harm. The culprit was never found. I have his snare hanging up in my shed!

Look for fox-runs; they are easy to spot, particularly when there is snow lying, and ascertain those places where the creature goes through hedges. The snare must be anchored firmly, the loop small enough to catch the fox by the head and not round its body.

Remove all human scent from your snares by wearing gloves when setting and smear earth round the wire. This also serves to dull them and prevent them from glinting on moonlight nights. You need patience; sometimes you may be lucky and catch a fox the very first night but more often your snare will wait a week before catching. Where snares are knocked over this could be because you are not setting them at the right height. Beware badgers; if you accidentally catch Brock then you must free him immediately. The easiest way to do this is to pin him down with a strong forked stick whilst you cut the snare off him with a pair of wire-cutters. Badgers are immensely strong and are ferocious when caught so make sure that you have the animal secured before attempting to cut the snare.

Mark the positions of your snares carefully. The best way is to tie a piece of string to the hedge above where each wire is set. Count carefully how many snares you put out, make sure that you check the same number twice daily, and when you come to remove them ensure that you do not inadvertently leave one behind.

Gassing

I would not encourage the amateur to attempt to gas fox earths. Cymag gas can be lethal, a faint whiff can make you vomit. It is also an uncertain method because you do not know for sure if the fox is below ground and if a vixen is aware that you have found her earth she will move her cubs elsewhere during

A fox cub, the scourge of the free-range poultry farmer. (Photo: Lance Smith)

the short time in which you have gone to fetch the gas. If an earth is in evidence and you decide to gas it, contact the Ministry of Agriculture for advice.

Cage traps

I know of people who have had incredible success catching foxes in cage traps, which to me dispels the myth about the creature's cunning. One person I know made a trap out of ten baker's trays wired together and has caught over a hundred foxes in six years! This is something I am now seriously considering because I never sleep easy when I have snares set. My greatest worry is that one of our cats will be caught. A cage can be left set 365 days a year and any domestic animal caught in it can be released unharmed.

Poison bait, of course, is illegal.

Shooting

I have never disputed that hunting foxes with hounds is humane. The cruelty aspect used by the anti-hunting protestors is a weak argument. The fox is killed quickly by the pack before being torn apart. I just wish that a lot more foxes were accounted for in this way.

Shooting is also humane provided that heavy shot (Nos. 3, 1 or BB) is used and foxes are shot within killing distance. This is something which must be instilled into all those taking part in fox-shoots.

Fox-shooting could well be the opening to some regular rough-shooting for the beginner. Particularly in upland areas where hunting on horseback presents difficulties, opportunities for fox 'clubs' exist. They are not clubs as such but rather a gathering of sportsmen who find their chosen sport in the pursuit of Reynard with guns. Mostly the gathering is an informal one taking place most weekends from about the middle of October right through to March. Hill-farmers welcome them for the fox presents a very real threat to their livelihood and a club may have permission to shoot over several hundred acres.

From my own experience on 'shoot days' clubs are always short of beaters and guns. Whilst there is an enthusiastic nucleus of participators the bulk of the turn-out is from casuals; forestry workers, farm labourers, virtually anybody who enjoys the thrill of the chase. But there never seems to be a full complement and as such much of the ground is unable to be beaten out properly, or else the guns are sparse and the foxes seem to know the safe places to break.

The obvious place to make contact with this form of shooting is in your local hostelry. Usually on Saturday evenings the fox-shooters will gather here to discuss the day's sport and maybe plan the morrow's. Your best approach is to offer your services as a beater but be prepared for a hard slog, for it will differ very much from the conventional beating on pheasant shoots. The terrain will be almost impenetrable in places for this is where Reynard's fortress is, in the heart of dense conifer thickets or patches of gorse, often on steep hillsides which offer a challenge to the hiker even on the narrow twisting sheep tracks. You will most certainly need to wear thornproof clothing, even if you sweat heavily in it, and in some places you will virtually have to crawl.

Virtually any breed of dog is acceptable on these shoots so long as it is not afraid of thick cover. It matters not whether the dog runs in to shot or even how wild it is, for the idea is to create as much disturbance within those thickets as possible to move the foxes out to the waiting guns. And the foxes will not bolt easily; often they will try to double back behind the beaters and dogs when there is not a full turnout of either. You need to make as much noise as possible, if you can borrow a hunting horn blow it to your heart's content. Or failing that a football rattle is excellent. You will need a stout stick to tap trees and thrash your way through clumps of undergrowth.

Fox-shooting is a slow and patient business for the gun. He may stand all day in atrocious weather conditions and not get a shot, maybe not even catch sight of a bolting fox. But he must not relax his vigilance, for the fox, going on ahead of beaters and dogs, will be wary. He will scent the guns and when finally he breaks cover it will be in full flight heading for the next patch of woodland. If you have put your gun down to light a cigarette or drink a cup of coffee from your flask you will have no time for a shot and the beaters' efforts will have been wasted.

Organisation is the key to successful fox-shooting and *safety must be a priority*. There may be as many as twenty guns to cover a stretch of woodland ride half a mile long. They should be placed at fifty yard intervals *with their backs to the beaters*. This is a double safety measure; they will be shooting *away* from the beaters and also any foxes which bolt will be taken in front, eliminating the dangerous practice of shooting 'down the line' in a moment of excitement. If there are enough guns then every fox which bolts will be within 25 yards of the nearest gun. It will be a matter of snap-shooting before your quarry reaches the next patch of cover.

Silence is essential and it is preferable not to smoke for the fox will certainly scent your tobacco smoke. There will be frequent long waits when nothing seems to be happening. You can hear the beaters and dogs in full cry but there is not a sign of a fox. Your attention can lapse, and in a moment of day-dreaming there is a flash of reddish-brown and a fox breaks. If you think you have hit one but it carried on, get the dogs on the scent the moment they appear.

For some years there has been a lucrative market in fox pelts. There are several firms of furriers who buy these, both wet and dry, for export to the continent. Often a good winter pelt, unmarked and skinned properly, can fetch up to £20. A poor, badly flayed one may only realise £2 or £3. The fox clubs rely on these pelts for their income, a return for their outlay – cartridges, clothing and vehicles – and one cannot begrudge them this bounty money. Often this has been the subject of criticism in the sporting press but logically it is better to reap some reward from a vermin species which needs to be controlled than to leave the carcasses to rot.

The argument is that the price of pelts encourages all and sundry to set wires, many amateurishly set where they might catch domestic animals and only be inspected at irregular intervals. There will always be an undesirable element out to reap a profit from any sport and it is up to the genuine fox-shooter to be on the lookout for the casual snarer, and to reprimand him if he is not following the code of practice laid down.

Foxes have to be controlled and those who brave the elements during the winter months earn their share of the pelt money. They are the gamekeepers in remote areas where there are no official keepers.

Rough-shooting

When fox-shooting, it is not permissible to shoot at any other species, even vermin, except a fox. A free-for-all vermin shoot combined with a fox-drive would result in too much gunfire which would deter the main quarry as well as presenting a safety hazard. Those guns lining the edge of a wood are concerned only with Reynard, so placed that they will be firing against a safe background. A rabbit bolting down the line would result in a deviation from the procedure and shots might be taken at any angle.

However, there are occasions when the fox-club is invited to have a day at rabbits and other vermin. This is the way farmers reward them for the foxes they have killed. The sport may take the form of a semi-organised rough-shoot, a line of guns walking the fields, dogs working the cover. Or perhaps there will be walking guns and standing guns alternately in an attempt to provide some driven shooting. Again safety is paramount; you must take care not to shoot towards the opposing line or take a shot in thick cover where you cannot see.

All game must be respected. The land over which you walk could well be let to a syndicate or to a private tenant and your sport must not be at the expense of that which is rightfully the shooting tenant's.

Sometimes rabbits are shot after dark using a pick-up truck. One or two foxes are accounted for in this way as well but, as stated earlier in this book, this type of shooting should not be carried out on a regular basis.

Fox-shooting could be the door to some fairly regular vermin shooting for he who has not yet found some sport of his own. It all depends in which part of the country you live. Fox-clubs are mostly to be found in Wales and its borderlands, and mountainous country in the north, those parts of Great Britain where hunting on horseback is not practicable.

Years ago the shooting of foxes was a taboo subject. Gamekeepers killed them in secret and buried the corpses, for their hunting employers would probably have sacked them for such sacrilege. On the other hand the keeper might have lost his job if the pheasants were not in abundance on shooting days. He had to be deceitful if he was to be successful and remain in employment. Thankfully today landowners are more flexible in this matter and leave it to their gamekeeper's discretion.

Have no fear, Reynard will not become extinct. He has survived where his relative, the wolf, has succumbed to man the hunter. He will always survive but for the sake of the species itself and the rest of the wildlife in our countryside, we need to control the fox extensively.

CHAPTER THIRTEEN

Mixed Shooting

So far we have covered most of the possibilities where the enthusiast might obtain the shooting of his choice. We have looked at the basic quarry species but there are a few more which he might encounter.

Hares

Many years ago I remember my father travelling down to Suffolk each February for the annual hare-drive on a large estate. On his return his shoulder would be badly bruised; sometimes he shot with two guns and a loader. The total bag was in the region of 500 and he described the drives as akin to a flock of sheep coming towards you.

In latter years the hare population has been in decline. We read that investigations into this are in progress but, to me, the reason is abundantly clear. I have already mentioned the 150 dead hares being picked up within a radius of one and a half miles where paraquat spraying had been carried out. This chemical is widely used to check weed-control throughout Britain and if it can kill hares in one county it can kill them elsewhere. Yet nobody seems prepared to make a definite stand on the subject, to stand up and be counted. We read of inane comments to the effect that 'it is a pity we cannot educate hares not to graze within three hours of spraying'! An awful lot of farmers have been indoctrinated with an obsession with weeds. They are encouraged by the chemical companies to use more of this to kill that, to eradicate natural plant life on which the soil depends. Mineral deficiencies result in sick livestock but still the madness continues. It is up to the shooting fraternity to make their views known, to lobby their MPs to press for bans and restrictions on harmful herbicides and insecticides. We are in serious danger of losing the hare; if it does not become extinct then it will surely become a protected species.

The brown hare is a beautiful creature and although its greatest sporting attributes are to be seen in coursing it is, nevertheless, a worthy quarry for the shooting man. It is a master at the art of camouflage and often the walking gun will not spot a hare until it springs up in front of him on a bare field. It is up to full speed in a matter of yards and will leave a gundog standing.

Hares are large animals and will carry shot for some considerable distance if not hit in a vital place. For walked-up hares I would advocate No. 4 or 5 shot, no smaller, and all shots should be taken at a maximum of 30 yards.

Driven hares are a different proposition. They are coming towards you and present a head shot that is closer by the second. No. 6s will kill them outright.

I have not shot a hare for two seasons now. My reasons are twofold. First, there is a shortage of hares up in the hills surrounding my home. Secondly, neither of my daughters care for eating them whilst the rest of the family are quite happy to have jugged hare, which means we have to plan a hare meal when the girls are away, which is not all that often. Consequently a couple of joints in the freezer are likely to remain there an awful long time. So until the hare population shows a marked revival I will continue with my self-imposed ban.

Hares should be left intact and only gutted when they are skinned. Again, how long you hang them is a matter of personal choice. For myself the meat is quite strong enough when freshly killed so I generally prepare them for the freezer within twenty-four hours of shooting.

The hare population has declined in recent years. (Photo: Calvin Williams)

Mountain hares

The mountain hare is a much smaller animal than the brown hare and in appearance it resembles the rabbit. Its habitat is the mountainous regions of Scotland and is also to be found at high altitudes in Cumbria. Rarely does it come down below an altitude of 1,500 feet.

In the Scottish Highlands it is regarded as a pest. It is to be found in abundance amongst the rocks, living in clefts, and during the winter months its staple diet is lichen.

With the approach of cold weather its fur gradually loses its summer grey and turns white, with the exception of the ears which remain black. This process takes place without a moult. During the middle of September the feet begin to change colour but the total transformation is not complete until about the middle of November.

The mountain hare is a wild creature and is not easily approached. One day the moor may seem alive with these animals, the next there is scarcely one to be seen. Often this is due to the attention of birds of prey, particularly the golden eagle which is its chief predator. When there are eagles about the hares will seek cover amidst the rocks and remain there until all is clear. Foxes, too, take a toll of their numbers, but their worst enemy is the blizzards.

Shooting may be obtained through personal contact. If you happen to meet a Highland shepherd and the conversation turns to hares you could be lucky. This flockmaster will bemoan the grass they eat, which is the staple food of his sheep and sparse enough on high ground. He may well give you permission to try your luck but it will not be easy. The hares will be up and away before you get within a hundred yards of them and your best plan is to walk upwind and work your dog amidst rocky outcrops.

The meat of the mountain hare is inferior to that of its brown cousin and is generally only used for soup. Even during the meat shortages of the last war poulterers found that blue hares did not sell. Nevertheless, this creature offers some worthy sport and the chance to shoot in a truly wild environment. And at the same time you will be doing the sheep farmer a service in reducing its numbers. It is estimated that the creature grazes one third as much as a sheep!

Grouse and blackgame

Grouse and blackgame are not beyond the reach of the beginner. That Forestry Commission shoot which we considered earlier could well be an upland stretch of land purchased with a view to planting in the future. In the meantime the grouse and blackgame will remain because, as yet, the heather which is their staple diet has not been destroyed.

These birds of the wild moorlands rely upon the shoots of young heather for survival. This is only attained by regular muir-burning; patches of heather are selectively burned in the early spring, the old shoots destroyed to make way for new ones. This is the basis of moorland management, and where heather has been neglected and allowed to grow densely there will be few birds.

Up until a hundred or so years ago grouse were shot over pointers. An exciting method of walking-up, these excellent dogs freezing when they scented a covey, allowing the guns to approach within range before flushing the birds. Then in the latter half of the nineteenth century grouse-shooting became much more intensive; gamekeepers were employed upon the moors and driving became the accepted way of shooting. Permanent butts were built, heather was burned in rotation each spring and the keepers concentrated on reducing the vermin. Foxes and corvines are the worst enemies of grouse, particularly the hoodie crow.

Yet pointers did not disappear entirely from the scene and latterly are regaining their popularity, particularly the German short-haired pointer and now the Hungarian Visla.

The grouse population has declined since the war and nobody really knows the reason. Whilst newly afforested areas have certainly destroyed a proportion of the natural habitat this is not solely the reason because there are still extensive moors which are ideally suited to grouse which no longer produce the numbers of yesteryear. The Game Conservancy are engaged upon extensive research into this but the problem still remains much of a mystery.

Where there are few grouse they are best walked-up for they will not warant a team of beaters. Culling is necessary to produce healthy stock and a happy medium must be struck between under-shooting and over-shooting. Unfortunately grouse cannot be hand-reared in the manner of pheasants and partridges so re-stocking of moors does not have a simple solution. Birds must be encouraged to breed in the wild; vermin must be controlled, the habitat must be kept undisturbed and there has to be an abundance of grit at all times for this is very necessary to the grouse's digestion.

Grouse movements are often determined by the weather. Coveys can be in abundance in the heather one day and seeking shelter amidst the rocks the following if there is a downpour. Shoot your birds in the early part of the season for by October they are generally wild and when walking-up you will be lucky to get within gunshot of them.

Blackgame are large grouse, and are to grouse what pheasants are to partridge; you will more often find them singly than in coveys, they are strong fliers and excellent eating. The female is known as the greyhen. I shot my first on the moorlands thirty miles from Dumfries on a hotel shoot during a wildfowling holiday.

Snipe

You are likely to come across snipe on any boggy patch on your rough-shoot and they have a habit of showing up in the most unexpected places. I have seen them flushed out of kale fields and from the most insignificant of ditches where they have been feeding.

Snipe are unpredictable and provide the most testing of shots. One day there will not be any sign of them, the next you may flush a dozen or more off an irrigation ditch. There is an old saying that when you are flighting duck, 'the snipe come before the duck'. On my own shoot I have found that to be the reverse, snipe dropping in to feed on the marshy field long after the duck have finished coming and it is too dark to see. On my walk back home they are getting up everywhere in the pitch darkness.

I generally go for snipe in the middle of the day, particularly if there has been a hard frost and the stream is the only open water. The latter is narrow and twisting and one may expect a shot at any of the bends. A colleague of mine always lets off a shot on stepping on to the marsh, claims that it makes the birds lie close but I have never had any real proof to substantiate this. The secret is a stealthy approach, the dog kept at heel.

There are two schools of thought on snipe-shooting:

1. Fire the moment the bird springs.
2. Wait until the snipe has finished its initial jinking and then shoot.

Personally I always use the first method. The aerobatics of this small wader can be awe-inspiring to the novice but if you keep your eyes fixed on the bird and shoot quickly it is little different from shooting any other winged quarry. He who hesitates is lost! Do not think about its erratic flight, do not become indoctrinated by all that you have read or heard about its elusiveness in the air. Psychology is a major factor in most areas of the sport and none more than in snipe-shooting. Have belief in yourself and you will shoot well. Confidence is the key to success.

Snipe are superb eating. I try and build up a stock in the freezer and on occasions my wife and I have a couple on toast for supper, washed down with a bottle of home-made wine. On one occasion we invited some friends round for a snipe supper and although they had never eaten snipe before they were suitably impressed.

Snipe is something to savour rather than to devour hungrily. Roasted (head and innards removed!) and served with either toast or croutons, it has a delicate gamey flavour of its own, quite different from woodcock.

Capercaillie

Only the more fortunate of shooters are likely to meet up with this bird which is, in effect, the wood-grouse. Its staple diet is conifer shoots and although it

Marshy ground, ideal for snipe. (Photo: Lance Smith)

can become a pest in areas of commercial forestry there is usually a substantial levy per head charged. I heard of a man locally who went north to shoot capers and he bagged a brace which cost him £250!

Ptarmigan

Ptarmigan are almost always found above the snow line in mountainous regions of Scotland. They are found amongst the screes and peaks on terrain that is mostly frequented by mountain climbers, and the pursuit of this particular quarry requires more than average physical fitness.

This bird is rarely found below 2,000 feet. In spring the plumage is brown and grey, becoming more predominantly grey in autumn as the change begins to take place, turning white in winter except for a little black on the tail and wings. As with the mountain hare, Nature provides her own camouflage.

The ptarmigan's food consists of lichen, berries, seeds, moss and leaves. Its wariness, combined with tricky shooting conditions on rocky mountain slopes, makes it a worthy quarry, one which the sportsman may well consider having mounted by a taxidermist.

CHAPTER FOURTEEN

Overall Conservation

We cannot, and must not, attempt to segregate conservation from shooting. Only the antis will try to do this, for the most part relying upon misconstrued information which the media often seem to pay more attention to than the true facts. Likewise governments are sometimes contradictory in their approach to environmental welfare. The controversial issue of acid rain is a case in point.

Acid rain is brought about by pollution in the atmosphere, due to industrial fumes, exhaust fumes, power stations and a host of other causes. It *can* be reduced by the use of filters and other technological equipment which the majority of EEC countries are attempting to do. The EEC's attempts to reduce exhaust fumes by modifying the system in cars did not meet with co-operation from Great Britain who stubbornly stuck out for a much cheaper and less effective method.

According to the World Wildlife Fund there are 18,000 lakes in Sweden which are acidified to some extent and much of that pollution comes from other countries! Acid rain is detrimental to all living creatures, affecting wildlife through soil and water. Rich, loamy soils soak up and, to some extent, neutralise the acidity but on poor soils and bare rock the pollution quickly drains into the waterways. As a result streams, lakes and rivers are polluted which in turn affects fish, waterfowl, and all creatures which drink from that water.

Although these may seem to be factors beyond the control of fieldsportsmen there is something they can do. They can write to the press, lobby their MPs and perhaps join the Friends of the Earth. Although not a shooting organisation, the Friends of the Earth concentrate on preserving the environment in every way possible which makes them a major voice in the conservation area. They wage unceasing war on chemicals on the land, pollution in all forms, and anybody interested in learning more about them should write to:

Friends of the Earth,
377 City Road,
London EC1 1NA

Shooting and conservation are inseparable. (Photo: Lance Smith)

or alternatively to:

The Soil Association,
86–88 Colston Street,
Bristol BS1 5BB

The shooting man is not just concerned with the conservation of his legitimate quarry species but the environment as a whole. We talk frequently of the balance of nature but this incorporates the whole countryside; we cannot segregate specific areas. Plantlife, fish, trees, birds, animals, they all make up the rural scene and their welfare is our duty.

WILDLIFE AND COUNTRYSIDE ACT, 1981

This act is a complex one, there are many grey areas and it will be years before the initial dust-cloud has settled. In the meantime we must look at how the Act has affected the fieldsportsman, what changes it has brought about in the shooting field.

Neither the Act itself, nor the severe weather provisions, are applicable to Northern Ireland and the new provision in respect of deer applies to England and Wales only. The existing Game Laws have not been changed.

Protection of birds

All birds, their nests and eggs, are protected except Schedule 2 species listed earlier in this book, which are granted open seasons and may be killed or taken by legitimate methods.

The shooting season dates for quarry species, also listed in Schedule 2, have not been changed. However, some former quarry species have been given protection and are therefore no longer listed in this Schedule. These species now protected are:

White-fronted Goose   Long-tailed Duck
  (Scotland only)   Scaup
Bean Goose   Curlew
Whimbrel   Bartailed Godwit
Common Scoter   Grey Plover
Velvet Scoter   Redshank
Garganey   Jack Snipe

Pest species

The following pest species prior to the Act could be legally killed in certain areas but in future can be controlled only under terms of a licence under Section 16 of the Act. These species are:

Cormorant	Rock Dove
Goosander	Shag
Oystercatcher	Stock Dove
Red-breasted Merganser	

Taking eggs of wild birds

It is no longer legal to take the eggs from a wild duck's nest to hatch under a broody hen or in your incubator.

Prohibited methods of killing wild birds

Schedule 2 species may not be killed by the following methods:

1. Bows or crossbows
2. Explosives other than firearm or shotgun ammunition

However, a Section 16 Open General Licence allows the full use of semi-automatic weapons for the killing of pest species. These weapons are defined as having a magazine which is not capable of holding more than two rounds. In effect this means that it is legal to use a semi-automatic gun which has been blanked-off so that the magazine holds two cartridges with a third round in the chamber.

Sale of dead wild birds

Prior to the Act the sale of dead wild birds, legally taken, during the open season, was permissible. Now the Act prohibits the sale of *all* dead wild birds except those which are listed in sections 2 and 3 of Schedule 3. Part 2 of Schedule 3 lists those birds which may be sold dead at all times:

Woodpigeon	Feral pigeon

Part 3 of Schedule 3 lists those birds which may be sold dead from 1 September to 28 February:

Capercaillie	Pochard
Coot	Shoveler
Tufted Duck	Snipe
Mallard	Teal
Pintail	Wigeon
Golden Plover	Woodcock

The sale of dead wild geese was prohibited long before the Act came into force. Game are still covered by the Game Laws.

Exceptions

Prior to the Act a number of defences could be used by, for instance, a farmer shooting a protected species in order to protect his crops, i.e. a barnacle goose. Now he is required to apply for a licence. There is now a defence for a game rearer against prosecution for killing a protected bird which is damaging species kept for the provision or improvement of shooting and fishing. This defence would not apply in respect of Schedule 1 species, i.e. golden eagle, goshawk, all harriers, red kites, merlin, barn owl, peregrine. Species falling *within* this defence are: sparrowhawk, tawny owl, little owl and buzzard.

POINTS OF SPECIAL NOTE FOR GAMEKEEPERS

Protection of mammals

It is an offence to use a self-locking snare. Free-running snares are permissible but must be inspected at least once every day. The author has recommended earlier in this book that they are looked at twice a day.

It is illegal to set any trap or snare or to lay any poison or stupefying bait (e.g. alpha chloralose) for the purpose of killing any wild animal listed in Schedule 6: badger, wild cat, hedgehog, pine marten, otter, polecat, red squirrel. It is also an offence to kill any of these with an automatic or semi-automatic weapon, any device for illuminating the target (lamps or headlights), gas, sound recording (decoying by recorded calls) or mechanically propelled vehicles.

However, as a defence against prosecution for the sportsman unfortunate enough to be caught up in a legal wrangle whilst going about legitimate pest control, he should attempt to show that the purpose was to kill an animal which could be legally taken and that all reasonable precautions had been taken to prevent harm falling to Schedule 6 species.

There has been legislation following the Act concerning *badgers*. Nowadays the onus is on the defendant to prove that his intention was not to kill or harm badgers.

Rabbits and hares

The Act makes it lawful for the occupier of land, or persons authorised by him, to kill rabbits and hares at night provided he has written authority from any other person who is entitled to take these species on the land. It is also legal for these other persons to shoot rabbits and hares at night.

Sheep-worrying dogs

It is illegal to allow a dog to be at large (i.e. not on a lead or under close control) in a field where there are sheep. The exceptions are the dogs of the owner or occupier of the land, hounds out hunting and working gun dogs.

Deer

It is an offence to use a smooth bore weapon against deer but there are exceptions. Deer may be shot with a shotgun on cultivated land or enclosed woodland provided that a 12-bore firing a single non-spherical slug or AAA shot is used. This exception applies only where shooting is necessary for preventing damage to crops or property.

Releasing birds into the wild

It is an offence to release into the wild any bird or animal which is not normally resident in, nor a visitor to, Great Britain in a wild state. Specific species are listed in Schedule 9:

Capercaillie	Chukar Partridge
Carolina Wood Duck	Rock Partridge
Mandarin Duck	Bob White Quail
Canada Goose	Certain Ornamental Pheasants
Egyptian Goose	

Enforcement and penalties

Some of the penalties are increased to a maximum fine of £1,000. Constables are now permitted to stop and search any whom they suspect of committing an offence whereas previously they could only do so with those found committing an offence. The police may enter any land, other than a dwelling house, for this purpose and magistrates are able to award a search warrant for the police to enter premises if there are reasonable grounds for suspecting that an offence is to be found there.

The Wildlife and Countryside Act, 1981 comprises *four* separate parts covering wildlife, nature conservation, countryside and national parks, public rights of way and also a section on miscellaneous and general provisions.

Whilst the author has attempted to summarise the parts of the Act relevant to the shooting man, the sportsman would benefit from purchasing a copy of the Act, Chapter 69, published by HMSO at £6.35. It is important to understand this Act for ignorance of the law is no excuse for breaking the law.

SEVERE WEATHER ARRANGEMENTS

This again is merely a summary of the procedure which applies for the suspension of shooting during severe weather.

These are based on the state of ground data collated daily by thirteen coastal meteorological stations. This information is passed on to the Nature Conservancy Council who consult other organisations, including the BASC, and then advise the Secretary of State for the Environment when a statutory suspension of the shooting of wildfowl, golden plover, woodcock, snipe, coot and moorhen should be signed.

After seven days of severe weather has been recorded at seven or more of the meteorological stations, or ten days including one or two days of thaw, the BASC will notify the secretaries of clubs, joint councils and syndicates that if there is no let-up in the hard weather for another six days and no sign of a thaw, a statutory order suspending shooting is likely to come into effect. Information will also be given of where notice of such an order will appear. The order will be signed on the thirteenth day of severe weather but there will be a two day publicity period before the order comes into force at 0900 hours on the fifteenth day.

The Department of the Environment will seek the co-operation of the press, radio and television in an attempt to bring the notice of the suspension of shooting to all sportsmen. The BASC will also inform its affiliated clubs, joint councils and shooting clubs by telephone and set up a twenty-four-hour telephone information service, as well as issuing press announcements to local and national newspapers.

The order will be in force for a maximum of fourteen days but should there be a thaw in the meantime the BASC will notify all sources should the ban be lifted. If, however, the hard weather continues then the Secretary of State may be advised to renew the suspension for a further fortnight.

In many cases the experienced wildfowler has no need of a statutory order; he implements his own 'ban' and stops shooting once it is obvious that the birds are short of food and are no longer worthy quarry. A few days of severe weather can bring good sport but once the quarry are beginning to suffer from climatic conditions then it is totally unjustifiable to take advantage of them. I once heard of a bag of sixty geese being made by a party of shooters in the severe winter of 1962/63 when the birds resorted to feeding close to the shore on a frozen saltmarsh. No true sportsman would condone such a slaughter.

Sites of Special Scientific Interest

Controls over land which is noted for conservation importance are designated Sites of Special Scientific Interest. Although these areas were notified to Local

Planning Authorities as far back as 1949, the Wildlife and Countryside Act, 1981, upgraded them. The Nature Conservancy Council is responsible for advising landowners and tenants of these sites.

In recent years the drainage and reclamation of many of our marshlands has been detrimental to wildfowl, destroying valuable habitat, and in this respect SSSIs are invaluable to conservation. But we need to look much closer to see how the shooting man will be affected.

The Nature Conservancy Council has taken on the task of informing all landowners and tenants of such sites (including shooting tenants) of anything which they may consider is detrimental to conservation. This may include the felling of woodlands, spinneys, bulldozing out of hedges, drainage of natural wetlands. But it may also include the killing of any wild animal which the NCC considers not to be in the interests of conservation even if the said species is harmful to the shooting scene. They may even consider that the rearing of pheasants is not conducive to that particular environment. In which case shooting on SSSIs may well be under threat. Once a shooting tenant has been formally advised that the land over which he shoots has been designated a SSSI then he no longer has his former freedom to build-up his shoot how he sees fit. Anything he wishes to do in the way of management which concerns, for example, the making of flight ponds, the cutting of woodland rides and a host of other 'alterations', then permission must be requested in writing. It may or may not be granted. Reasons for refusal are not obligatory. Any normal shoot management operation might be considered as 'damaging'. He may require a 'notice of consent' before he can commence re-stocking with pheasants.

Shooting and conservation can go hand-in-hand provided both parties are willing to co-operate. Almost 70 per cent of the areas used by BASC affiliated wildfowling clubs in England are of SSSI status and many thousands more acres privately owned.

There should be no conflict. This information is given for the benefit of 'first-time' shooting tenants. If they enter into any agreement, written or verbal, then they must be aware of what is required of them on an SSSI designated shoot. It is hoped that co-operation will be mutual for conflict will benefit nobody. But conservation *is* important and whilst one must be seen to be doing one's share, the rights of the shooting man must not be whittled away. The environment, together with our sporting heritage, must be preserved for the benefit of future generations.

Finding shooting is only the beginning; from then onwards one has to build on the initial foundations and become a naturalist as well as a sportsman. The one is complementary to the other.

Index